100
BEST-SELLING
ALBUMS OF THE
50s

100
BEST-SELLING
ALBUMS OF THE
50s

Charlotte Greig

HOTHOUSE

This book is published by Hothouse
An imprint of Igloo Books Ltd
Henson Way, Telford Way Industrial Estate
Kettering, Northants, NN16 8PX
First published in 2004
hothouse@igloo-books.com

ISBN: 1-84561-004-0

Editorial and design by:
Amber Books Ltd
Bradley's Close
74-77 White Lion Street
London N1 9PF
United Kingdom
www.amberbooks.co.uk

Editorial or design queries should be addressed to Amber Books Ltd

Project Editor: Tom Broder
Design: Colin Hawes
Picture Research: Natasha Jones
Consultant: Roger Watson

Printed in Singapore

ACKNOWLEDGEMENTS

Thanks to HMV (hmv.co.uk) for their help in researching and supplying the albums featured in this book

Thanks to the following for help with supplying the albums as well as for their invaluable industry knowledge:
Reckless Records (www.reckless.co.uk), Islington, London
Flashback (www.flashback.co.uk), Islington, London
Golden Grooves (www.goldengroovesrecords.com), Old Street, London
Haggle (www.hagglevinyl.com), Islington, London
The Music and Video Exchange, Notting Hill, London
Stage and Screen, Notting Hill, London
Beanos (www.beanos.co.uk)

Contents

Editor's foreword

The ranking of the 100 best-selling albums of the 1950s listed in the following pages is based on a combination of the number of gold and platinum sales awards each album has achieved, the position the album reached on the Billboard chart and the length of time it spent in this position. Greatest hits and compilation albums – such as Elvis Presley's compilations of his hit singles – are not included, though live albums and original movie and musical soundtracks do feature.

The RIAA awards

The gold and platinum sales certifications used to rank the best-selling albums in this book are awarded by the Recording Industry Association of America (RIAA). An RIAA gold award represents sales of at least 500,000 albums and a platinum award sales of at least 1,000,000 albums. In a decade from which accurate records for album sales rarely survive, the RIAA awards represent one of the most consistent and reliable measures of sales success, providing an effective way to rate the relative position of the best-selling albums.

These figures also have the advantage – unlike lists based purely on chart position – of showing album sales from the date of first release right up to the present day, meaning the success of an album such as Miles Davis' *Kind Of Blue*, which failed to chart in the 1950s but has sold well in every decade since, is reflected in its position.

Chart position

The 1950s were the early days of albums and sales were relatively low compared to those of later decades. Only 65 albums from this period have officially been certified gold or platinum, so the rankings below that in this list are largely dependent on data from the Billboard charts.

Billboard magazine first began running its weekly albums chart in 1955, meaning the ranking of albums in the list with sales of less than 50,000 is weighted towards those released in the second half of the 1950s. Nonetheless, there are a number of albums released before 1955 that still charted strongly. Mantovani's 1953 album *Christmas Carols*, for example, first charted in 1957 and continued to make regular appearances on the albums charts until 1962.

While the information provided by the charts can't provide the exact sales figures for each album, it does identify those albums that were the decade's strongest sellers and provides a way to rank them relative to one another. Where one or more albums achieved the same peak position, the length of time each album spent in this position is also taken into account.

Facts and figures
The appendices provide a breakdown of some of the most interesting facts and figures found throughout this book. You can find out which artists have the most albums in the list and which were the most successful bands and solo artists. You can see which albums received one of the new-established Grammy awards and which contain the most Number Ones. You can discover what the best-selling movie and musical soundtracks were and which record labels were the most successful of the decade.

Alongside tributes to old favourites there are enough surprises to keep the most dedicated music buff guessing and stimulate plenty of lively discussion. Elvis Presley's epochal debut album, for example, was outsold by Henry Mancini's soundtrack to the TV detective series *Peter Gunn*. None of Sinatra's albums, despite their popularity today, rank as highly as Johnny Mathis' now more neglected album *Heavenly*.

The entries are illustrated using a mixture of US and UK sleeve designs – a selection that includes some of the most iconic images of the decade.

Sinatra has more albums in the 100 best-selling albums than any other artist. His 1959 release *Come Dance With Me* also won him two Grammy awards, including Best Album.

The Best-Selling Albums of the 1950s

The 1950s album charts represent the last phase of popular music before rock 'n' roll took over. Seen from one perspective, the range of this music – from Rodgers and Hammerstein to Frank Sinatra, from Mantovani to Mitch Miller – is the sound of a lost era. From another, it's a reminder of a time when popular music was in its infancy and only just developing, in terms of artists, formats and market, into the multi-million dollar industry it is today.

The birth of the album

Prior to the 1950s, the recorded-music market was dominated by the 78-rpm record, a brittle disc made out of shellac. This was generally 10 inches in diameter and capable of holding around three minutes of music on each side (a limited number of 12-inch discs, which could hold up to five minutes of music, were also available). The 78 rpm disc was enough for two pop songs or dance tunes, but if the consumer wanted to buy a longer work – say a classical concerto or a collection of all the songs from a musical – the only option was to buy a set of three to six 78s cased in paper sleeves and bound together in a cardboard or leather book.

These sets became known as 'albums' because, with their paper sleeves bound in book form, they looked similar to a photographic album.

The triumph of the long player

In 1948, the Columbia record label developed a revolutionary new format, replacing the old, easily breakable, shellac records with more flexible 10- or 12-inch vinyl records that had narrower grooves and could play at 33$\frac{1}{3}$ rpm. These new discs, known as 'long players' or 'LPs', revolutionized the market. RCA responded by launching a smaller 7-inch vinyl format, which played at 45 rpm; these were known first as 45s, then as 'singles'. RCA also continued with the photograph album format by making box sets of four or five singles, which they marketed as a more compact alternative to Columbia's new LPs.

The simplicity of putting on one record for 20 minutes per side rather than continually juggling half-a-dozen shorter discs meant that Columbia's long players soon won out over the RCA box sets, and by the middle of the decade the market had settled on the formats it would retain for the next 30 years. Buyers had a choice between 45-rpm singles (sometimes also available as 78s) and 33$\frac{1}{3}$ rpm long players, which were increasingly referred to as 'albums'.

By 1955, the LP or album market had established itself to such a point that *Billboard* magazine, which had been producing a singles chart since 1936, began running a weekly albums chart as well.

Different markets

The music made for the new albums market in the 1950s was altogether different from that produced for the singles market. As far as the record companies were concerned, singles were predominantly for teenagers and children. They also catered to the tastes of less well-off adults; black music and country music were both predominantly released on singles. The album charts during the 1950s represented the tastes of the more wealthy section of the American public. This was partly based on simple economics – albums cost more than two dollars to buy, singles under a dollar – but it was also a legacy of earlier decades, in which longer classical works had needed to be released as 'albums'.

For a while, there was an assumption that albums would be aimed at an older audience, and would include classical music, jazz and the easy-listening end of pop. Rock 'n' roll artists, by contrast, would rarely make albums unless they

1950s albums were generally targeted at the older, more conservative music-buyer, a fact that goes some way to explain the predominance of light-orchestral music such as Mantovani's *Strauss Waltzes*.

were Elvis or Pat Boone and even then they would be markedly less successful than they were in the singles charts. Thus, where in later decades the album charts came to reflect the latest sounds in popular music, in the 1950s they overwhelmingly reflected the tastes of older, more conservative record buyers.

The best-sellers

The list of the decade's best-selling albums certainly shows this to be the case. There are no less than 20 soundtrack albums from film and theatre productions, and nine Christmas albums. As for individual artists, Frank Sinatra is the dominant figure, with ten albums in the list. Johnny Mathis and Harry Belafonte are not far behind with six entries apiece, while Elvis Presley only has five albums in the list.

The popularity of light orchestral music – what we now call easy listening, MOR, or even muzak – is also striking. Mantovani has six entries in the best-selling albums of the 1950s, Jackie Gleason has four albums and Ray Conniff and Roger Williams have three entries each. Some of these artists, like Mantovani and his orchestra, were from the classical tradition, offering string-laden orchestral versions of classical works and show tunes. Other musicians, like Ray Conniff or Billy Vaughn, were the descendants of the big-band

explosion of the 1930s, and offered listeners a more syncopated take on the pop standards.

Even more surprising is the popularity of the band leader and record-company mogul Mitch Miller's series of family 'sing-along' albums, which occupy six places in the charts. Yet when one considers that these records (which came complete with lyrics sheets to allow the listeners to join in) were the karaoke entertainment of their day, their success doesn't seem quite so odd.

Rock 'n' roll rebels

Even a cursory glance at the best-selling albums of the 1950s confirms – with the striking exceptions of Elvis Presley and Miles Davis – that this is not a list of musical innovators. Instead, it points to the fact that the top-selling music of a period is not always what is best remembered by posterity or discussed by critics.

The popular image we now have of the 1950s – rock 'n' roll, jazz and James Dean – actually represents aspects of the culture that at the time were the exceptions. If you want to know why James Dean became a rebel without a cause, you just need to look at the album charts. The reason why rock 'n' roll was such a sensation becomes plain: it's because mom and pop were busy listening to Mantovani, Johnny Mathis, Ray Conniff and Tennessee Ernie Ford.

The King rules

Revealingly, the highest-ranking album from the decade's pre-eminent artist, Elvis Presley, is not his epochal self-titled debut album but his *Christmas Album*. The reasons this album comes out on top are twofold. First, Christmas albums were perennial favourites, often outselling an artist's more original work. Second, Elvis specialized in recording singles, and many of his most successful albums were compilations of hit singles (which are not included here).

Another intriguing inclusion, high in the list is Miles Davis's jazz masterpiece, *Kind Of Blue*. Uniquely among the Top-100 albums, this never made the charts at the time. While most of the records here were strong sellers when they first came out, *Kind Of Blue* has stayed in the catalogue and gains fresh devotees with each passing year – to the extent that it has now sold over 3,000,000 copies in the US and continues to sell thousands more each week, more than 40 years after its initial release. Only Dave Brubeck's *Take Five* comes near its success as a jazz classic that has become a long-term bestseller.

Movies and musicals

Another perennial favourite of 1950s album buyers were the soundtracks to stage and movie musicals. The stage musical may have been

Elvis' Christmas Album, with it's emphasis on seasonal good cheer rather than teenage rebellion, was better suited to the tastes of the album-buying public than his more rock 'n' roll releases.

coming towards the end of its golden age in the 1950s, but you'd never have thought so at the time. *West Side Story*, *The King & I*, *South Pacific* and *The Sound Of Music* all appeared during the decade, each one full of memorable songs that have become permanent staples of the popular-music repertoire. The popularity of the musical is certainly reflected in the list of the decade's best-selling albums, with the Broadway production of *My Fair Lady* and the movie version of *Oklahoma!* both appearing in the Top Five.

Cool to croon

After the musicals, we come to the crooners. Johnny Mathis had the biggest hit albums of the 1950s, but his star has waned significantly in subsequent decades. Mathis was originally signed by Columbia A&R boss Mitch Miller as a replacement for Frank Sinatra, whom Miller detested and sacked from the label. For a while, Mathis was every bit as popular as Sinatra; posterity, however, has come down firmly on the side of Sinatra, whose hit albums of the decade are almost all still in print.

Sinatra is a key figure in the development of the album market, and not just because of his popularity. Sinatra was the first pop artist to really see the potential of the album as a format in its own right. Where other crooners would put

out albums that consisted of a couple of hit songs plus a mass of filler, each of Sinatra's 1950s albums recorded for the Capitol label were expressly conceived of as albums. Thus *Songs For Swingin' Lovers* consists of uptempo love songs, *In The Wee Small Hours* is about heartbreak and loss, while *Come Fly With Me* features tunes with a travel theme.

Designs on the decade

Another reason Sinatra's albums were so influential was the attention paid to their covers. For the first years of record retailing 78s were sold in plain paper or cardboard sleeves that carried the name of the record company and nothing else. Stores kept them behind the counter and the purchaser had to ask for the record by name. This only began to change in 1938 when a young graphic designer named Alex Steinweiss, who was working for Columbia, designed an eye-catching box cover for their album-style release of *Smash Song Hits Of Rodgers & Hart*. Later on, when Columbia started releasing LPs it was Steinweiss who invented the folded, printed and laminated cardboard sleeve that became the standard packaging for albums.

Steinweiss' lead was quickly followed in the jazz field, where labels like Blue Note and Prestige created memorable album sleeves throughout the 1950s. In the sphere of popular music, though, it was Frank Sinatra's covers that led the way in demonstrating how the artwork on the outside could complement the music on the inside – something we now take for granted.

Calypso and folk

As well as Sinatra, the other great male solo artist was Harry Belafonte, whose gentle calypso style was a sensational success in 1950s America. At a time when African-American artists, from Little Richard to Billie Holiday, received little or no attention from mainstream white audiences, Belafonte became a huge star.

Another musical movement to hit middle America in the late 1950s was the folk boom. Confronted by the space age, America was starting to look back to its roots in search of something reassuringly traditional. Step forward the Kingston Singers, whose easy, humorous take on folk music made them one of the hottest acts of the late 1950s. Even Mitch Miller took notice of the folk boom, recording *Folk Songs Sing Along With Mitch*.

Heavenly sounds

Rock 'n' roll may have been the devil's music, but religion was winning the battle of the album charts. Apart from Elvis Presley, there are only

Sinatra's recordings for Capitol were intended to be more than just collections of songs. Albums such as *Songs For Swingin' Lovers* were designed with a consistent theme in mind, both in terms of content and packaging.

two rock 'n' roll artists to make an impression: Ricky Nelson and Pat Boone. Conversely, never have so many explicitly devotional recordings made the charts. Tennessee Ernie Ford had four hits with his albums of hymns and spirituals. Not far behind came the Mormon Tabernacle Choir with *The Lord's Prayer* and the Robert Shaw Chorale's album of *Christmas Hymns*.

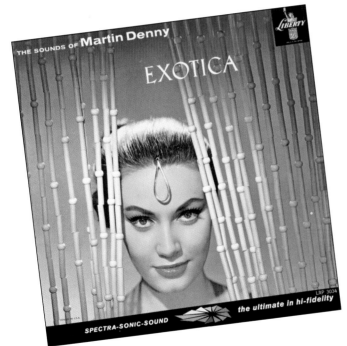

The strange sound effects and bird calls on Martin Denny's album *Exotica* were perfectly suited to the new stereo technology of the era.

At this time, classical music could still make an impact on the album charts. The pianist Van Cliburn spent seven weeks at the top of the charts with his recording of Tchaikovsky's Piano Concerto, which had won him the first prize at the Moscow Tchaikovsky competition at the height of the Cold War. The conductor Antal Dorati also did well with a technically-innovative recording of *Tchaikovsky's 1812*, which was of particular appeal to hi-fi buffs.

Music goes 'stereo'

It wasn't just the record formats that were changing in the 1950s, but the equipment they were played on as well. The new buzzword was 'stereo'. For the first time, the technology was there to split the audio signal in two. Suddenly, anyone who could afford a stereo hi-fi set-up could transform their living room into a miniature concert hall. And it was in classical and light orchestral music that the potential of this new technology was first grasped. Mantovani experimented assiduously with microphone placement, and Mercury's *Living Presence* series, of which Dorati's recording of *Tchaikovsky's 1812* was one of the first examples, showed just what the new recorded sound was capable of.

Indeed, at least one of the records here – Martin Denny's *Exotica* – owed its success as much to its demonstration of the possibilities of stereo as to its unlikely mixture of light jazz and mock-Hawaiian folk music. Curiously enough, Denny's *Exotica* has, in recent years, had something of a revival, its kitsch appeal making it a hit with the lounge music revivalists of today. That's an honour it shares with the series of Jackie Gleason romantic mood-music albums, which were another one of the more unlikely successes of the decade.

Cool and comfortable sounds

The 1950s albums charts, then, were not the sound of teenage rebellion – they were the sound of middle America kicking back after the trauma of World War II and enjoying a new era of unprecedented prosperity. The 1950s did see a number of revolutionary developments that would transform the record industry and popular culture forever: the new sounds of rock 'n' roll were starting to emerge into the mainstream and the technological advances of the era began to reveal what recorded music was capable of. But this was also a time when most album buyers prized the familiar over the radical. Rock 'n' roll may have ruled the singles charts, but for most listeners it was the enchanting show scores, the pop-standards and the easy-listening favourites that truly defined the sound of the decade.

TV star Jackie Gleason was a virtual non-musician who didn't even play on his records, but his series of easy-listening albums clearly struck a chord with the album-buying public. The sleeve to *Lonesome Echo*, Gleason's first album to make Number One, was designed by Salvador Dali.

100 Fanny

| • **Album sales:** Under 500,000 | • **Highest position:** 7 | • **Release date:** January 1955 |

Fanny was the biggest hit of Broadway veteran Harold Rome's career. Rome had success before the war with his left-wing revue *Pins And Needles*, and became fashionable again following the success of 1954's *Wish You Were Here*, which ran for 598 performances and gave Eddie Fisher a Number One hit with the title song.

As with *Wish You Were Here*, the book for *Fanny* was written by Joshua Logan, who also directed. *Fanny* tells the story of a Marseilles waterfront girl whose lover goes off to sea in search of adventure. It starred Florence Henderson (later to find fame as Carol Brady in *The Brady Bunch*) as Fanny, and Ezio Pinza (the long-term principal bass for the Metropolitan Opera) as the father of the young man. The show's secret weapon, however, was the Turkish belly-dancer Nejla Ates, whose routine, shocking for the times, became a regular showstopper (so much so that, for publicity purposes, Broadway showman David Merrick had a life-size nude statue of her installed in Central Park).

Opening in November 1954, *Fanny* ran for an impressive 888 performances and, on release in 1955, the album of the cast recording reached Number Seven on the album charts.

Number One singles:
None

Grammy awards:
None

Label: US: RCA Victor

Recorded in: New York, USA

Personnel:
Florence Henderson
Ezio Pinza
Nejla Ates
Walter Slezak
William Tabbert

Producer:
Morris Stoloff

1 Overture (5:03)
2 Octopus Song (1:06)
3 Restless Heart (2:48)
4 Never Too Late For Love (2:13)
5 Cold Cream Jar Song (0:28)
6 Why Be Afraid To Dance? (3:38)
7 Shika, Shika (2:27)
8 Welcome Home (3:25)
9 I Like You (2:35)
10 I Have To Tell You (2:09)
11 Fanny (1:55)
12 Panisse And Son (2:27)
13 Wedding Dance (2:07)
14 Finale Act I (0:52)
15 Birthday Song (2:22)
16 To My Wife (2:13)
17 The Thought Of You (2:05)
18 Love Is A Very Light Thing (2:10)
19 Other Hands, Other Hearts (1:48)
20 Montage (2:32)
21 Be Kind To Your Parents (2:21)

Total album length: 49 minutes

ORIGINAL CAST
RECORDING

RCA **V**ICTOR ®
LOC-1015

DAVID MERRICK and JOSHUA LOGAN

present

EZIO **PINZA**   WALTER **SLEZAK**

A NEW MUSICAL

"FANNY"

Musical Play by

S. N. BEHRMAN and JOSHUA LOGAN

Music and Lyrics by

HAROLD ROME

(based on the trilogy of Marcel Pagnol)

Directed by

JOSHUA LOGAN

A "NEW ORTHOPHONIC" HIGH FIDELITY RECORDING

Sleeve artwork by Zinn Arthur

© RCA Printed in U.S.A.

B.G. In Hi-Fi

| • **Album sales:** Under 500,000 | • **Highest position:** 7 | • **Release date:** March 1955 |

Bandleader Benny Goodman ('The King of Swing') was some way past his heyday by the mid 1950s. The late 1930s had been the time when he dominated the singles charts, but the coming of war had sounded a death knell for the big bands and even Goodman had been forced finally to disband his permanent outfit in 1949.

B.G. In Hi-Fi was the product of Goodman's excitement with the possibilities of the new studio recording technology. Tired of reissuing old material, he decided to re-record some of his best-loved numbers in hi-fi, working at Riverside Studios in New York. Half the album's 16 tunes, including the likes of 'Let's Dance' and 'Stompin' At The Savoy', feature his big band (for the most part playing Fletcher Henderson arrangements).

The remaining eight songs, including a high-speed rendition of 'Get Happy', feature two smaller bands, between them boasting an array of talent that includes Ruby Braff and Charlie Shavers on trumpets, Jo Jones on drums and Goodman himself on clarinet.

The result was an album that ranks with Goodman's finest recordings and reached Number Seven in the charts.

Number One singles:
None

Grammy awards:
None

Label: US: Capitol

Recorded in: New York, USA

Personnel:
Benny Goodman (d. 1986)
Ruby Braff
Jo Jones
Mel Powell
Charlie Shavers
Bobby Donaldson
George Duvivier

Producer: N/A

1   Let's Dance (2:13)
2. Air Mail Special (3:36)
3   Get Happy (3:03)
4   Jersey Bounce (3:03)
5   When I Grow Too Old to Dream (3:23)
6   You Brought a New Kind of Love to Me (2:49)
7   Blue Lou (2:49)
8   Jumpin' at the Woodside (3:28)
9   Stompin' at the Savoy (3:13)
10 Sent for You Yesterday (And Here You Come Today) (3:03)
11 (What Can I Say) After I Say I'm Sorry? (3:08)
12 Rock Rimmon (3:26)
13 You're a Sweetheart (2:59)
14 Somebody Stole My Gal (3:24)
15 Big John's Special (3:06)
16 Let's Dance (2:55)

Total album length: 50 minutes

Benny Goodman

98 | There's No Business Like Show Business

| • **Album sales:** Under 500,000 | • **Highest position:** 6 | • **Release date:** December 1954 |

There's No Business Like Show Business was one of the most lavish film musicals of the 1950s, the era of the big screen productions. MGM had dominated the genre for years, and with this film 20th Century Fox were determined to outdo them. To this end they assembled a formidable package.

The songs were by Irving Berlin – essentially a collection of some of his greatest hits, from 'Alexander's Ragtime Band' and 'When the Midnight Choo Chooo Leaves for Alabam' to the showstopping title track – rather than a newly composed score. The stars included Marilyn Monroe at the height of her career, Broadway diva Ethel Merman and teen idol Johnny Ray.

The flimsy story concerns the trials and triumphs of a vaudeville family as they attempt to make their way in show business. Critics suggested that more of Fox's budget might have been spent on providing a better script, but the set-piece musical numbers were at the real heart of the film, so the soundtrack did not suffer.

Unfortunately, for contractual reasons Monroe's parts had to be re-recorded on the soundtrack album by Dolores Gray. Nevertheless, the album as a whole was catchy and appealing enough to reach Number Six in the charts.

Number One singles:
None

Grammy awards:
None

Label: US: Decca; UK: Brunswick

Recorded in: N/A

Personnel:
Ethel Merman (d. 1984)
Donald O'Connor (d. 2003)
Dan Dailey (d. 1978)
Mitzi Gaynor
Johnnie Ray
Dolores Gray
20th Century Fox Orchestra and Chorus

Producer: N/A

1 There's No Business Like Show Business (2:31)
2 When The Midnight Choo Chooo Leaves for Alabam (1:54)
3 Play A Simple Melody (2:51)
4 After You Get What You Want, You Don't Want It (3:37)
5 If You Believe (3:19)
6 A Man Chases A Girl (Until She Catches Him) (5:15)
7 Lazy (5:26)
8 Heat Wave (4:24)
9 Sailor's Not A Sailor ('Til A Sailor's Been Tattooed) (4:41)
10 Alexander's Ragtime Band (8:38)
11 Finale (2:23)

Total album length: 45 minutes

Original Soundtrack

20

Selections from the Sound Track of Darryl F. Zanuck's presentations of

IRVING BERLIN'S
THERE'S NO BUSINESS LIKE SHOW BUSINESS
A 20th Century - Fox Production in Cinemascope

LYRICS and MUSIC by
IRVING BERLIN

PRODUCED BY
SOL C. SIEGEL
DIRECTED BY
WALTER LANG
COLOUR BY
DELUXE

ETHEL MERMAN

DONALD O'CONNOR

DAN DAILEY

JOHNNIE RAY

MITZI GAYNOR

and
DOLORES GRAY
(not in film)

with THE 20TH CENTURY-FOX ORCHESTRA and CHORUS
ALFRED NEWMAN and LIONEL NEWMAN, Musical Directors   KEN DARBY, Vocal Director

THERE'S NO BUSINESS LIKE SHOW BUSINESS • AFTER YOU GET WHAT YOU WANT YOU DON'T WANT IT • PLAY A SIMPLE MELODY
LAZY • WHEN THE MIDNIGHT CHOO CHOO LEAVES FOR ALABAM' • IF YOU BELIEVE • A MAN CHASES A GIRL • HEAT WAVE
A SAILOR'S NOT A SAILOR • ALEXANDER'S RAGTIME BAND • THERE'S NO BUSINESS LIKE SHOW BUSINESS (Finale)

Brunswick   LONG PLAYING MICROGROOVE
FLEXIBLE RECORD

LONG
33⅓
RPM
PLAYING

LAT 8059

97 Damn Yankees

| • **Album sales:** Under 500,000 | • **Highest position:** 6 | • **Release date:** June 1955 |

The soundtrack of this musical was written by Richard Adler and Jerry Ross, who had previously had successes with *Rags To Riches* and *The Pyjama Game*. The pair had become well known for using American speech idioms in songs that were closely bound to the plot, and in *Damn Yankees* they continued in this style.

The story of *Damn Yankees* was based on the book *The Year the Yankees Lost the Pennant* by Douglas Wallop. It tells of a middle-aged baseball fan who sells his soul in a Faustian pact with the Devil, and becomes a young baseball star. However, in keeping with the original tale, there is a price to be paid.

Highlights of the show included the songs 'Whatever Lola Wants', 'Two Lost Souls' and 'Heart'. Gwen Verdon played the feisty female lead role of Lola, the Devil's assistant, giving a performance that made her name and earned her a Tony Award. She later went on to star in the film version of the show.

Damn Yankees opened at the 46th Street Theatre in May 1955 and ran for 1019 performances. After hitting Number Six, the album recording of the original cast remained in the charts for 12 weeks.

Number One singles:	Personnel:
None	Gwen Verdon (d. 2000)
	Stephen Douglass
Grammy awards:	Ray Walston
None	Robert Shafer
Label: RCA Victor	**Producer:** N/A
Recorded in: N/A	

1   **Overture: Six Months Out Of Every Year** (4:44)
2   **Goodbye, Old Girl** (3:16)
3   **Heart** (4:42)
4   **Shoeless Joe From Hannibal, Mo** (3:42)
5   **A Little Brains, A Little Talent** (3:39)
6   **Man Doesn't Know** (3:11)
7   **Whatever Lola Wants** (3:12)
8   **Heart (Reprise)** (1:25)
9   **Who's Got The Pain?** (2:54)
10 **The Game** (4:32)
11 **Near To You** (3:29)
12 **Those Were The Good Old Days** (2:38)
13 **Two Lost Souls** (2:18)
14 **A Man Doesn't Know** (1:25)
15 **Finale** (0:58)

Total album length: 46 minutes

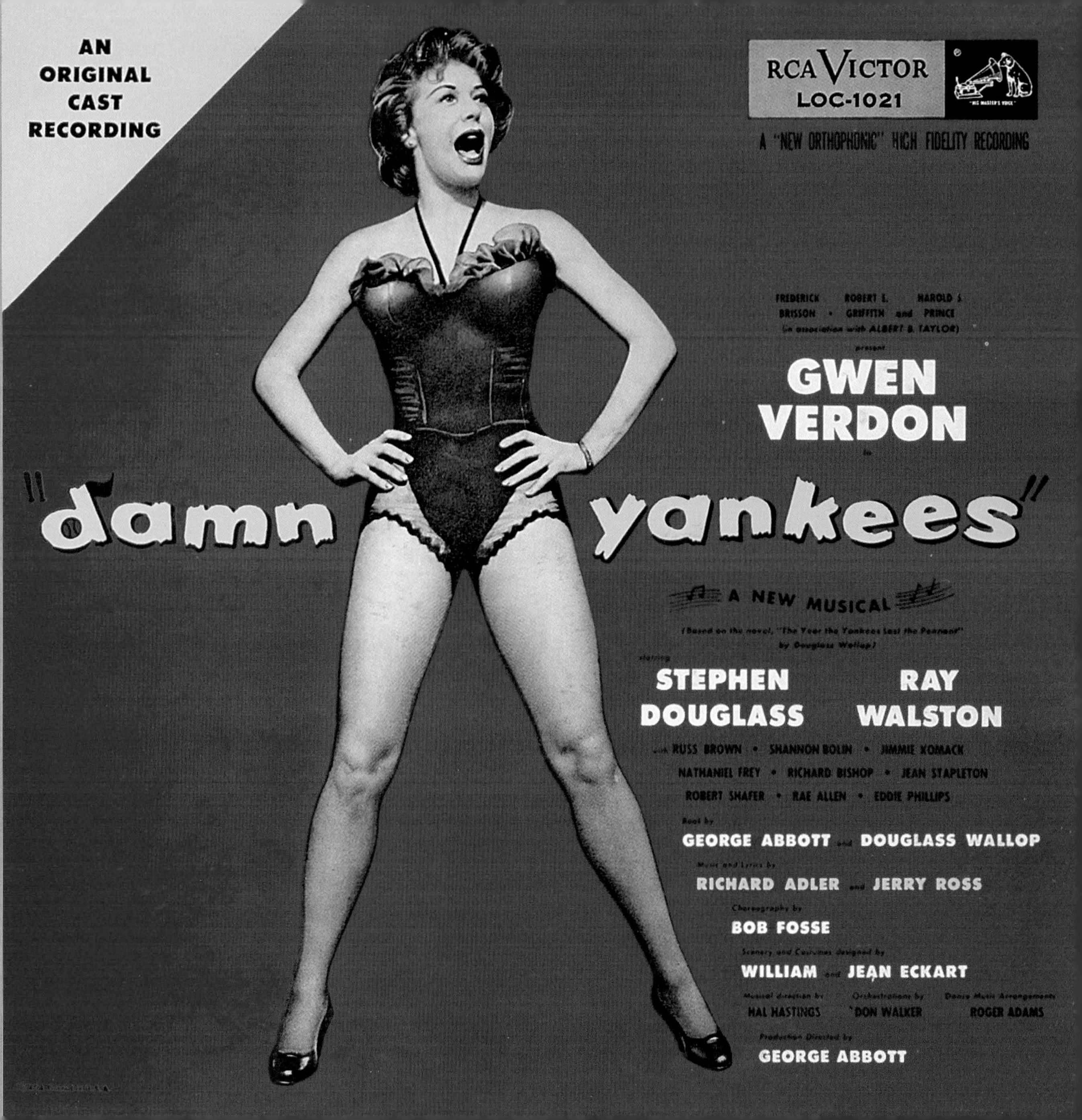

AN
ORIGINAL
CAST
RECORDING

RCA VICTOR
LOC-1021
A "NEW ORTHOPHONIC" HIGH FIDELITY RECORDING

FREDERICK   ROBERT E.   HAROLD S.
BRISSON • GRIFFITH and PRINCE
(in association with ALBERT B. TAYLOR)

present

GWEN
VERDON

"damn yankees"

🎵 A NEW MUSICAL 🎵

(Based on the novel, "The Year the Yankees Lost the Pennant"
by Douglass Wallop)

starring

STEPHEN   RAY
DOUGLASS   WALSTON

with RUSS BROWN • SHANNON BOLIN • JIMMIE KOMACK

NATHANIEL FREY • RICHARD BISHOP • JEAN STAPLETON

ROBERT SHAFER • RAE ALLEN • EDDIE PHILLIPS

Book by

GEORGE ABBOTT and **DOUGLASS WALLOP**

Music and Lyrics by

RICHARD ADLER and **JERRY ROSS**

Choreography by

BOB FOSSE

Scenery and Costumes designed by

WILLIAM and **JEAN ECKART**

Musical direction by   Orchestrations by   Dance Music Arrangements

HAL HASTINGS   DON WALKER   ROGER ADAMS

Production Directed by

GEORGE ABBOTT

96 Picnic

• Album sales: Under 500,000 | **• Highest position:** 6 | **• Release date:** May 1956

The film *Picnic*, directed by Joshua Logan, was a box-office success in 1955. When the soundtrack was released the following year, it went straight into the album charts.

The sensual film score, by George Duning, was a highlight of this screen adaptation of William Inge's original play. The story centred on the romance between a handsome, world-weary drifter, played by William Holden, and a pretty, small-town girl, played by Kim Novak. The theme of the movie, reflected in Duning's musical score, concerns the repressed sexuality and frustrated dreams of a small community in a Midwestern town. One of the most memorable aspects of the film for both critics and audiences was the scene in which William Holden and Kim Novak dance together to the strains of 'Moonglow'.

Playing the score for this and other popular tracks in the film, including 'Love's Theme', was the Columbia Studio Orchestra, conducted by Morris Stoloff. Although the film did not win an Oscar for best picture that year, it was critically acclaimed, and did very well at the box office. The soundtrack was also very successful, hitting the album charts at Number Six, and remaining in the charts for a total of 18 weeks.

Number One singles: None	**Recorded in:** N/A	
Grammy awards: None	**Personnel:** Morris Stoloff Columbia Studio Orchestra	
Label: US: Decca	**Producers:** N/A	

1 **Love's Theme** (2:34)
2 **Hal's Theme** (1:54)
3 **The Owens Family** (4:11)
4 **Flo And Madge** (4:25)
5 **Love Theme from 'Picnic'** (2:16)
6 **Moonglow** (3:45)
7 **It's a Blue World-Torn Shirt** (4:58)
8 **Torn Shirt** (6:32)
9 **Rosemary Pleads/Rosemary Alone** (2:10)
10 **Culmination/Hal's Escape** (5:52)
11 **That Owens Girl/Millie** (1:31)
12 **You Love Me/Madge Decides** (5:40)

Total album length: 44 minutes

DL 78320

FULL STEREO

MUSIC FROM THE SOUND TRACK

of the Columbia Picture

HI-FI
DECCA
RECORDS

picnic

95 Mantovani Stereo Showcase

| • **Album sales:** Under 500,000 | • **Highest position:** 6 | • **Release date:** January 1959 |

The enormous popularity of the light classical conductor and bandleader Annunzio Paolo Mantovani (Monty to friends and fans) during the 1950s was not just as a result of his shimmering arrangements of familiar tunes. Perhaps Mantovani's lasting influence is as a pioneer of recorded sound. Unlike other bandleaders and conductors of his generation, Mantovani realized that the making of a record had to be approached in an entirely different way to the performing of a live concert.

To that end he worked ceaselessly with the sound engineers at Decca's studios in London to find better ways of recording his orchestra. They became world leaders in the art of the microphone set-up, and when the new stereo technology came along they embraced it enthusiastically. *Mantovani Stereo Showcase* was just that, a showpiece in which Mantovani revisited some of his favourite themes, from 'Greensleeves' to 'Some Enchanted Evening', and set out to show just what stereo could offer. The result was an album that became a must have for owners of the new hi-fi systems.

Mantovani Stereo Showcase reached Number Six in the charts – a considerable achievement for a stereo-only release at a time when few people owned stereo equipment.

Number One singles: None	**Recorded in:** London, UK
Grammy awards: None	**Personnel:** Annunzio Paolo Mantovani (d. 1980)
Label: US: Decca; UK: London	**Producers:** N/A

1 **Theme From Limelight (2:55)**
2 **Village Swallows (3:15)**
3 **Tammy (3:35)**
4 **Come Prima (For The First Time) (2:40)**
5 **Greensleeves (3:15)**
6 **Schön Rosmarin (2:15)**
7 **I Could Have Danced All Night (3:00)**
8 **Some Enchanted Evening (3:30**

Total album length: 24 minutes

Mantovani

FULL FREQUENCY **STEREOPHONIC** SOUND

MANTOVANI

LONDON
FULL FREQUENCY STEREOPHONIC SOUND

SS 1

STEREO
Showcase

LIMITED **2⁴⁹** EDITION

THEME FROM LIMELIGHT
from FILM ENCORES—Vol. 1 (PS 124)

VILLAGE SWALLOWS
from STRAUSS WALTZES (PS 118)

TAMMY
from FILM ENCORES—Vol. 2 (PS 164)

COME PRIMA (For The First Time)
from CONTINENTAL ENCORES (PS 147)

GREENSLEEVES
from WALTZ ENCORES (PS 119)

SCHÖN ROSMARIN
from CONCERT ENCORES (PS 133)

I COULD HAVE DANCED ALL NIGHT
from GEMS FOREVER (PS 106)

SOME ENCHANTED EVENING
from SONG HITS FROM THEATRELAND (PS 125)

94 Music To Remember Her

| • **Album sales:** Under 500,000 | • **Highest position:** 5 | • **Release date:** April 1955 |

When actor and comedian Jackie Gleason first put the idea of an album of romantic mood music to Capitol, they were not altogether keen. It was only after Gleason promised to reimburse the record company personally for any losses incurred by the project that they agreed to go ahead. As it turned out, however, Gleason didn't need to dig into his pocket – the resulting album, *Music For Lovers Only*, was a huge hit and inspired a series of successful follow-ups.

The first of these to appear on the album chart was *Music To Remember Her*. On this release, Gleason came up with a cute gimmick: each song or tune had a different girl's name: Ruby, Cherry, Dinah, Sweet Lorraine, and so on. The music itself was smoothly unobtrusive, only Bobby Hackett's wistful cornet and trumpet parts rising above the restrained orchestration. This was a definitively mellow sound, for as Gleason liked to claim, 'the only thing better than one of my songs is one of my songs with a glass of scotch'. The record-buying public were quick to agree and the album reached Number Five in the charts during an overall stay of 16 weeks.

Number One singles:
None

Grammy awards:
None

Label: US: Capitol

Recorded in: N/A

Personnel:
Pete King
Bobby Hackett

Producer:
Jackie Gleason (d. 1987)

1 **Ruby** (3:22)
2 **Dinah** (3:06)
3 **Stella By Starlight** (3:45)
4 **Sweet Sue, Just You** (3:14)
5 **Marie** (2:36)
6 **Jeannine, I Dream Of Lilac Time** (3:05)
7 **Louise** (3:06)
8 **Tangerine** (3:27)
9 **Marilyn** (4:10)
10 **Diane** (2:34)
11 **Charmaine** (2:41)
12 **Laura** (3:28)

Total album length: 39 minutes

Jackie Gleason

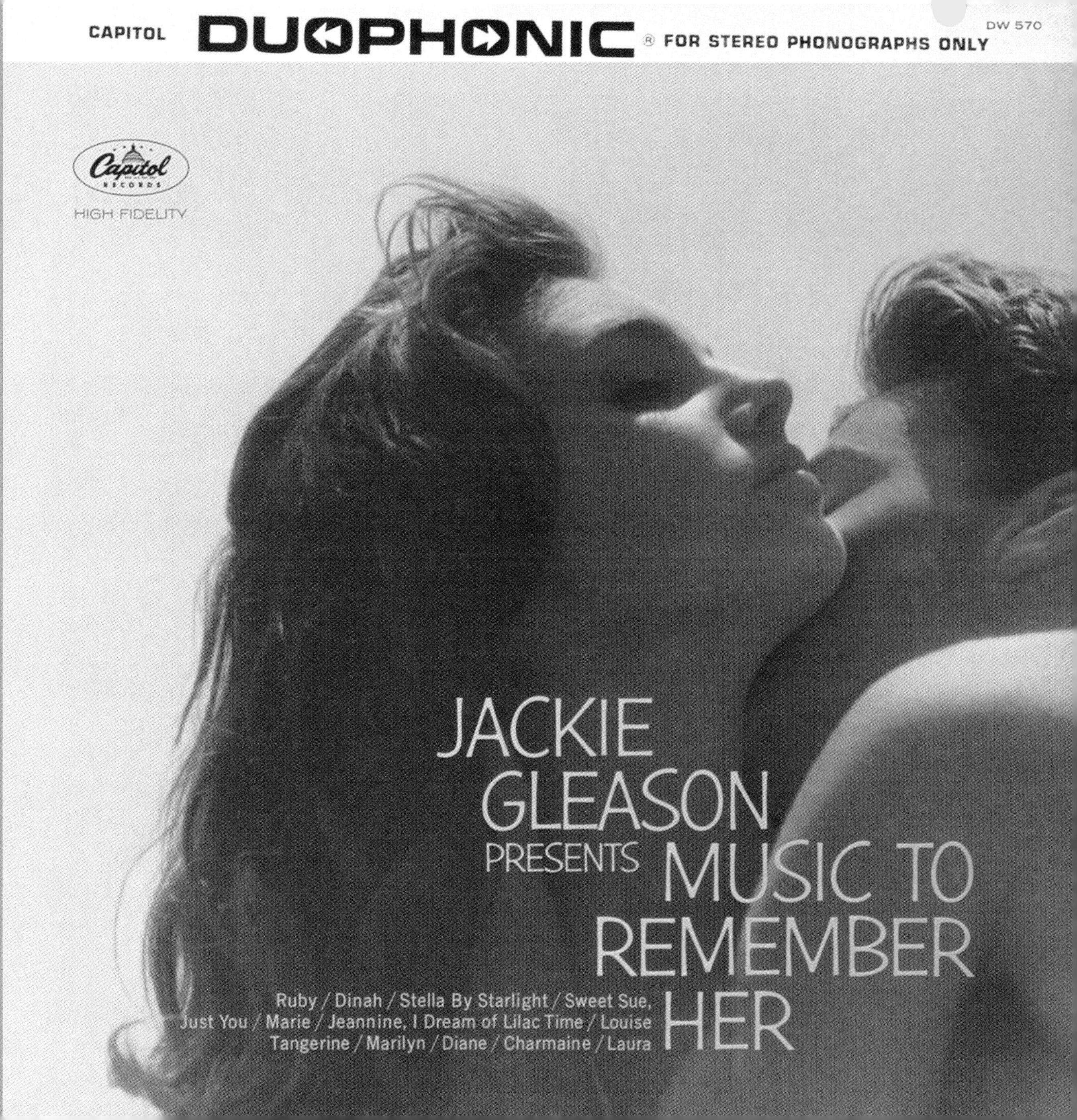

CAPITOL DUOPHONIC® FOR STEREO PHONOGRAPHS ONLY
DW 570
Capitol RECORDS
HIGH FIDELITY
JACKIE GLEASON
PRESENTS MUSIC TO REMEMBER HER
Ruby / Dinah / Stella By Starlight / Sweet Sue,
Just You / Marie / Jeannine, I Dream of Lilac Time / Louise
Tangerine / Marilyn / Diane / Charmaine / Laura

93 Miss Show Business

| • **Album sales:** Under 500,000 | • **Highest position:** 5 | • **Release date:** September 1955 |

Judy Garland's biggest hit album of the 1950s came in 1955, just as she was launching her comeback after her movie career had collapsed in the late 1940s, due to emotional turmoil. Her comeback had begun with rapturously received concert performances at the London Palladium and The Palace, New York. It continued with her Academy Award nomination for her first movie in four years, 'A Star Is Born', and was confirmed by her first starring TV special for CBS.

Miss Show Business is essentially a record of the songs she sang in that special, though these were recordings made beforehand in the studio to enable Capitol Records to rush the album into the shops just two days after the show aired. Under the guidance of her long-time collaborator Roger Edens, Garland began the set with a

choral number 'This Is The Time Of The Evening', following with a couple of medleys, one of vaudeville tunes and another of movie songs. However, the piece de resistance was the closing number, a rendition of 'Over The Rainbow' which had Garland sobbing by the end.

Capitol Record's canny marketing campaign ensured that the album was a hit, reaching Number Five on the US charts.

Number One singles:
None

Grammy awards:
None

Label: US: Capitol

Recorded in : Hollywood, USA

Personnel:
Judy Garland (d. 1969)
Jack Cathcart

Producer: N/A

1 **This Is The Time Of The Evening / While We're Young (4:48)**
2 **Medley: You Made Me Love You/For Me And My Gal/The Boy Next Door/The Trolley Song (6:16)**
3 **A Pretty Girl Milking Her Cow (3:03)**
4 **Rock-a-bye Your Baby With A Dixie Melody (2:38)**
5 **Happiness Is A Thing Called Joe (4:25)**
6 **Shine On Harvest Moon/My Man/Some Of These Days/I Don't Care (6:07)**
7 **Carolina In The Morning (3:04)**
8 **Danny Boy (3:05)**
9 **After You've Gone (2:14)**
10 **Over The Rainbow (3:31)**

Total album length : 39 minutes

Judy Garland

MISS SHOW BUSINESS

92 High Society

• **Album sales:** Under 500,000 | • **Highest position:** 5 | • **Release date:** 1956

The soundtrack to *High Society* was released in 1956. Starring Bing Crosby, Grace Kelly, and Frank Sinatra, the film was based on Philip Barry's stage play, *The Philadelphia Story*. Music and lyrics were by Cole Porter. Louis Armstrong also had a major role, appearing as leader of his jazz band. With such a stellar cast and score, the movie could hardly fail.

The story involves a society lady, played by Grace Kelly, who is planning to marry for the second time. Her first husband, played by Bing Crosby, hopes to change her mind. To complicate matters, two reporters, played by Frank Sinatra and Celeste Holm, have arrived to cover the wedding.

Cole Porter's light-hearted songs, together with witty dialogue from Barry's play, made this a frothy but very classy production. The hit songs from the Cole Porter score include 'Who Wants To Be A Millionaire', 'True Love', and 'Well, Did You Evah?'. Other highlights are 'High Society Calypso' and 'Now You Has Jazz', both featuring Louis Armstrong. The orchestration was by Nelson Riddle, with music direction from Johnny Green and Saul Chaplin.

The soundtrack reached Number Five in the Billboard album charts and stayed in the charts for a total of 28 weeks.

Number One singles:
None

Grammy awards:
None

Label: US: Capitol

Recorded in: N/A

Personnel:
Cole Porter Orchestra
Louis Armstrong (d. 1971)
 and His Band
Bing Crosby (d. 1977)
Frank Sinatra (d. 1998)
Celeste Holm
Grace Kelly (d. 1982)

Producers: N/A

1 High Society (Overture) (3:27)
2 High Society Calypso (2:11)
3 Little One (2:27)
4 Who Wants To Be A Millionaire? (2:03)
5 True Love (3:04)
6 You're Sensational (3:53)
7 I Love You, Samantha (4:28)
8 Now You Has Jazz (4:14)
9 Well, Did You Evah? (3:47)
10 Mind If I Make Love to You? (2:23)

Total album length: 32 minutes

Original Soundtrack

A NEW HIGH FIDELITY RECORDING FROM THE SOUND TRACK OF THE MGM PICTURE

"High Society"

Deep In My Heart

| • **Album sales:** Under 500,000 | • **Highest position:** 4 | • **Release date:** January 1955 |

Deep In My Heart was the last in a series of Hollywood biopics devoted to the lives of the great musical composers. Previous songwriters to be celebrated in this fashion had included Cole Porter, George Gershwin, Jerome Kern and Richard Rodgers. This time around, the songwriter was a slightly lesser known figure, Sigmund Romberg, the composer of operettas such as *The Student Prince* and *The Desert Song*, which had been big hits in the 1920s but out of fashion by the 1950s.

Previous biopics had tended to be lavish affairs that played fast and loose with the facts. However, this time writer Leonard Spigelglass stayed relatively faithful to the story of Romberg's life. Add a top-notch cast – José Ferrer, Vic Damone and Ferrer's then wife, Rosemary Clooney, among them – and the result was a film that worked as a story, as well as a sequence of musical production numbers.

The songs themselves stood up admirably. The libretto of the original operettas was adapted in such a way that numbers such as 'Softly, As In A Morning Sunrise' and 'Lover Come Back To Me' emerged as timeless standards, helping the soundtrack to reach Number Four in 1955 chart.

Number One singles:
None

Grammy awards:
None

Label: US: MGM

Recorded in: N/A

Producer: N/A

Personnel:
José Ferrer (d. 1992)
Helen Traubel
Howard Keel
Vic Damone
Rosemary Clooney
   (d. 2002)
Ann Miller
Jane Powell
Gene and Fred Kelly
Adolf Deutsch and the
   MGM Studio Orchestra

1   Overture
2   Leg Of Mutton Rag
3   Your Land And My Land
4   You Will Remember Vienna
5   It
6   Auf Wiedersehn
7   Serenade
8   Softly, As In A Morning Sunrise
9   Road To Paradise
10 Will You Remember (Sweetheart)
11 Mr And Mrs
12 I Love To Go Swimmin' With Wimmen
13 Lover Come Back To Me
14 Stout Hearted Men
15 When I Grow Too Old To Dream

Official times not available

Selections Recorded from the Sound Track of M-G-M's Colour Musical Sung by
José Ferrer
Helen Traubel
Rosemary Clooney
Tony Martin
Howard Keel
Gene and Fred Kelly
Ann Miller
Vic Damone
Jane Powell
Based on the Life and the Melodies of
SIGMUND ROMBERG
Deep in my Heart
M-G-M
LONG PLAYING
33⅓ R.P.M
RECORD
Songs
Serenade
Auf Wiederseh
Road to Paradise
Stout Hearted Men
Lover Come Back To Me
Your Land And My Land
Softly As In A Morning Sunrise
Will You Remember (Sweetheart)
When I Grow Too Old To Dream
I Love To Go Swimmin' With Wimmen . . . and other songs
M-G-M Studio Orchestra and Chorus Conducted by ADOLPH DEUTSCH

90 Peter Pan

| • **Album sales:** Under 500,000 | • **Highest position:** 4 | • **Release date:** April 1955 |

The soundtrack to the musical 'Peter Pan' hit the charts in early 1955, hot on the heels of its Broadway run. It's often reported to have been a Broadway flop, having only lasted a relatively meagre 152 performances, but in fact, the rights had already been sold to NBC TV. It was a pre-arranged plan that the show should close on Broadway after 19 weeks and the cast should then make the television version.

In the long term, it was the TV version that ensured that this production of J.M. Barrie's children's classic should become the definitive version for an entire generation of Americans. Starring in it was Mary Martin as Peter Pan. English light entertainer Cyril Ritchard gave a memorable performance as the delightfully evil

Captain Hook. The music was by Moose Charlap and Jule Styne, with lyrics by Carolyn Leigh, Betty Comden and Adolph Green.

The soundtrack album didn't simply fillet out the songs from the production, but also included snatches of plot and dialogue to give the listeners a potted version of the show as a whole. On release in 1955, the *Peter Pan* soundtrack reached Number Four in the charts during an overall stay of eight weeks.

Number One singles:
None

Grammy awards:
None

Label: US: RCA Victor

Recorded in: New York, USA

Personnel:
Mary Martin (d. 1990)
Cyril Ritchard
Kathy Nolan
Robert Harrington

Producer: N/A

1 Overture (3:30)
2 Prologue (1:56)
3 Tender Shepherd (2:00)
4 I've Gotta Crow (3:30)
5 Never Never Land (3:22)
6 I'm Flying (3:51)
7 Pirate Song (0:54)
8 Hook's Tango (1:26)
9 Indians (2:35)
10 Wendy (2:37)
11 Tarantella (0:56)
12 I Won't Grow Up (3:07)
13 Oh, My Mysterious Lady (3:28)
14 Ugg-A-Wugg (3:25)
15 Distant Melody (2:14)
16 Captain Hook's Waltz (2:53)
17 Finale (6:57)

Total album length: 49 minutes

Richard Halliday presents EDWIN LESTER'S PRODUCTION

MARY MARTIN
as
PeTeR PAN

with

CYRIL RITCHARD
In a New Musical Version of the Play by SIR JAMES M. BARRIE
Production Directed and Staged by
JEROME ROBBINS

Wonderful, Wonderful

• **Album sales:** Under 500,000 │ • **Highest position:** 4 │ • **Release date:** 1957 │

Johnny Mathis' sophomore album *Wonderful, Wonderful* was a breakthrough on several levels. His first album had been a straight jazz record, beautifully arranged by Gil Evans and others but apparently too sophisticated for a mass audience. Since then, Mathis had become a pop crooner with a string of hit singles arranged by Ray Conniff. For the new album though, rather than just assemble a collection of hits, Columbia label boss Mitch Miller had a more adventurous plan.

Wonderful, Wonderful was one of the first pop vocal albums designed to be listened to as an entity. Arranger Percy Faith was brought in to help craft it into a smooth, faintly jazzy confection that saw Mathis working his way through standards like 'That Old Black Magic' and 'All Through The Night'. The result was an album perfectly suited to late-night listening. None of Mathis hit singles were included – not even his 1957 'Wonderful, Wonderful' after which the album is rather misleadingly named.

Wonderful, Wonderful is still seen by many as Mathis' finest achievement. Though it didn't quite hit the commercial heights of some of his later albums, it reached Number Four in the charts and established Mathis as a top albums artist.

Number One singles:
None

Grammy awards: None

Label: US: Columbia; UK: Fontana

Recorded in: New York, USA

Personnel:
Johnny Mathis
Percy Faith and his
  Orchestra
Ernie Royal
Jimmy Abato

Producer:
Mitch Miller

1 Will I Find My Love Today
2 Looking At You
3 Let Me Love You
4 All Through The Night
5 It Could Happen To You
6 That Old Black Magic
7 Too Close For Comfort
8 In The Wee Small Hours Of The Morning
9 Year After Year
10 Early Autumn
11 You Stepped Out Of A Dream
12 Day In – Day Out

Official times not available

Johnny Mathis

Wonderful, Wonderful

JOHNNY MATHIS

The Late, Late Show

• **Album sales:** Under 500,000 │ • **Highest position:** 4 │ • **Release date:** February 1958 │

Very few genuine jazz albums made the charts during the 1950s and fewer still by genuine jazz singers. Only the perennial Louis Armstrong and the great Ella Fitzgerald were regular album sellers in the period. Billie Holiday never came near the charts and Dinah Washington didn't have a hit album until the 1960s.

So for a young Dinah Washington disciple called Dakota Staton to make the Top 10 with her first album was an extraordinary event. Partly it was down to the power of her label Capitol, then extremely hot with Frank Sinatra and Nat King Cole, that *The Late, Late Show* became a staple not just of jazz and R&B stations but also of pop radio. Partly it was that, first time out, Dakota Staton happened to put together a remarkably consistent and satisfying collection of songs. Backed by a top-notch small combo, she had the bluesiness of Dinah Washington allied to a youthful freshness. The songs are mostly standards but the title track, in particular, has become Dakota Staton's, while her take on 'My Funny Valentine' is considered another standout.

Released in late 1957 *The Late, Late Show* made it to Number Four, during an extended chart stay of some 41 weeks.

Number One singles:
None

Grammy awards:
None

Label: US: Capitol

Recorded in: Hollywood, USA

Personnel:
Dakota Staton (d. 2001)
Hank Jones
Jonah Jones
Van Alexander

Producer:
Dave Cavanaugh

1   Broadway (2:50)
2   Trust In Me (2:44)
3   Summertime (2:10)
4   Misty (2:35)
5   Foggy Day (2:18)
6   What Do You See In Her? (2:36)
7   Late Late Show (2:34)
8   My Funny Valentine (2:44)
9   Give Me The Simple Life (2:16)
10 You Showed Me the Way (2:48)
11 Moonray (2:42)
12 Ain't No Use (2:40)

Total album length: 31 minutes

Dakota Staton

SM-876

the late, late show

DAKOTA STATON

'Mark Twain' And Other Folk Favorites

| • **Album sales:** Under 500,000 | • **Highest position:** 3 | • **Release date:** 1956 |

Harry Belafonte's first full album was a collection of folk songs, many of which he had learned of from archives at the Library of Congress. Having started his career as a pop singer, it was clear from this recording that Belafonte had now changed direction and fallen in love with folk music, not only from the Caribbean, but from the American and European traditions as well.

Some of the songs on the album, such as 'John Henry' and 'Tol' My Captain', were African-American in origin. Others were West Indian, either traditional or original compositions. Yet others, like 'The Drummer And The Cook' and 'Lord Randall' harked back to the ancient ballads of the British folk tradition. Belafonte's original compositions included 'Man Piaba', a West Indian-styled song co-composed with Jack K. Rollins. It was a humorous account of a young man trying to find out about the 'birds and the bees'. Another Belafonte original was the title track, 'Mark Twain', a song about 19th-century workers on the Mississippi river boats.

The album was well received by the critics and sold well, climbing to Number Three on the Billboard album charts. It then remained in the charts for a total of six weeks.

Number One singles:
None

Grammy awards:
None

Label: US: RCA Victor

Recorded in: New York, USA

Personnel:
Harry Belafonte
Millard Thomas

Producers:
H. Winterhalter
Henri René
Jack Lewis
Joe Carlton

1   **Mark Twain** (3:44)
2   **Man Piaba** (3:31)
3   **John Henry** (3:29)
4   **Tol' My Captain** (2:45)
5   **Kalenda Rock** (3:23)
6   **The Drummer And The Cook** (2:03)
7   **The Fox** (2:50)
8   **Soldier, Soldier** (1:36)
9   **The Next Big River** (0:20)
10 **Delia** (2:58)
11 **Mo Mary** (2:14)
12 **Lord Randall** (4:08)

Total album length: 33 minutes

Harry Belafonte

Here's the Album that first brought Belafonte
fame and fortune...listen again as he sings

"MARK TWAIN"
and other folk favorites

Harry Belafonte

Mark Twain
Man Piaba
John Henry
Tol' My Captain
Kalenda Rock
The Drummer and the Cook
The Fox
Soldier, Soldier
The Next Big River
Delia
Mo Mary
Lord Randall

LPM-1022

86 Where Are You?

| • **Album sales:** Under 500,000 | • **Highest position:** 3 | • **Release date:** August 1957 |

Where Are You? was Frank Sinatra's third Capitol album of 1957, following on from the string quartet-backed ballad collection, *Close To You* and the uptempo *A Swingin' Affair*. This was another ballad collection, and the first of Sinatra's Capitol albums to be recorded without Nelson Riddle's arrangements. It was also Sinatra's first album to be recorded in stereo.

The new arranger was Gordon Jenkins whose lush string arrangements, and preference for a large orchestral backing, gave the album a more classical feel in comparison to Riddle's jazzier approach. That said, the choice of material and the rhythmic pacing does impart a strong blues feel, reminiscent of Billie Holiday at her most downbeat. The songs themselves are almost exclusively torch songs, including 'I'm A Fool To Want You', 'Lonely Town' and, a Billie Holiday favourite, 'I Cover The Waterfront'.

The determinedly melancholy *Where Are You?* didn't quite match the success of its predecessor, *A Swingin' Affair*, peaking one place lower in the charts at Number Three, but it still managed a creditable overall stay of 21 weeks which was enough to inspire Sinatra to re-unite with Jenkins to record a companion piece, *No One Cares*, two years later.

Number One singles:
None

Grammy awards:
None

Recorded in: Hollywood, USA

Label: US & UK: Capitol

Personnel:
Frank Sinatra (d. 1998)
Gordon Jenkins

Producer:
Voyle Gilmore

1 **Where Are You?** (3:28)
2 **The Night We Called it A Day** (3:25)
3 **I Cover The Waterfront** (2:56)
4 **Maybe You'll Be There** (3:04)
5 **Laura** (3:26)
6 **Lonely Town** (4:12)
7 **Autumn Leaves** (2:51)
8 **I'm A Fool To Want You** (4:50)
9 **I Think Of You** (3:02)
10 **Where is The One?** (3:10)
11 **There's No You** (3:46)
12 **Baby, Won't You Please Come Home** (2:59)

Total album length: 42 minutes

Frank Sinatra

Where are you?

WHERE ARE YOU?· THE NIGHT WE
CALLED IT A DAY· I COVER THE
WATERFRONT· MAYBE YOU'LL BE
THERE· LAURA· AUTUMN LEAVES· I'M A
FOOL TO WANT YOU· I THINK OF YOU·
THERE'S NO YOU· BABY, WON'T YOU
PLEASE COME HOME· ETC.

FRANK SINATRA

with **GORDON JENKINS** and his orchestra

85 Belafonte Sings Of The Caribbean

| • Album sales: Under 500,000 | • Highest position: 3 | • Release date: September 1957 |

After the huge success of his album *Calypso*, Harry Belafonte went on to present more West Indian songs on this album. Belafonte was a serious folk collector, and here he demonstrates his knowledge, singing a range of songs from the Caribbean islands.

Some of the tracks were written by Lord Burgess, who had penned hits for Belafonte in the past. However, there was also a humorous topical song, 'Love, Love Alone' by John Hardy, which commented on the abdication of the British king, Edward VII, to marry American divorcee Mrs Simpson. This kind of material, which forms an important part of West Indian calypso, had not been tackled by Belafonte before on disc.

In addition to showing the range of calypso songs, the album also expanded the accompanying instrumentation, with an orchestra conducted by Robert DeCormier (Bob Corman). Once again, a small, intimate combo of guitars, bass and drums was used, together with marimba, flute, clarinet, trumpet, and other jazz-flavoured elements of the Caribbean calypso sound. Lyrics to the songs were also made available in a companion booklet.

The album yielded a hit, 'Island In The Sun', which became the theme to the movie of the same name, starring Belafonte.

Number One singles:
None

Grammy awards:
None

Label: US: RCA Victor

Recorded in: New York, USA

Personnel:
Harry Belafonte
Bob Corman And His
 Orchestra
Millard Thomas
Franz Casseus
Victor Messer

Producer:
Joe Carlton

1 Scratch, Scratch (2:39)
2 Lucy's Door (3:43)
3 Cordelia Brown (2:53)
4 Don't Ever Love Me (2:46)
5 Love, Love Alone (3:19)
6 Cocoanut Woman (3:18)
7 Haiti Cherie (3:18)
8 Judy Drownded (3:28)
9 Island in the Sun (3:21)
10 Angelique (2:40)
11 Lead Man Holler (4:18)

Total album length: 36 minutes

LSP-1505

STEREO
Electronically Reprocessed

BELAFONTE
SINGS OF THE
CARIBBEAN

RCA VICTOR
A "New Orthophonic" High Fidelity Recording

Sleeve artwork by DC Gunn

84 Pal Joey

• **Album sales:** Under 500,000 | • **Highest position:** 2 (1 week) | • **Release date:** 1957

The soundtrack to *Pal Joey* is something of an oddity. On the one hand, it was recorded separately from the film, almost like a Sinatra solo album, at the Capitol Records studio in Hollywood with Sinatra's regular arranger Nelson Riddle. On the other hand, while Sinatra has half a dozen songs, there are also contributions from Jo Ann Greer and Trudy Erwin (dubbing songs that Rita Hayworth and Kim Novak appear to sing in the film). As it transpired this approach worked very well. *Pal Joey* reached Number Two on the US album charts and critics agree it is one of the best of Sinatra's soundtrack albums.

The movie itself is a film version of the classic Rodgers and Hart musical, with Sinatra playing the title role of Joey Evans, a womanizing nightclub singer. 'I Didn't Know What Time It Was', 'My Funny Valentine' and 'Bewitched' are the best-known ballads, the last two of which are sung by Sinatra, while 'The Lady Is A Tramp' suits Sinatra's uptempo style perfectly. The swinging reading of 'I Could Write A Book' that appears in the movie is replaced by a ballad reading on the album. The 1957 film, directed by George Sidney, received an Academy Award nomination for Best Sound.

Number One singles:
None

Grammy awards:
None

Recorded in: Hollywood, USA

Label: US: Capitol

Personnel:
Frank Sinatra (d. 1998)
Jo Ann Greer
Trudy Erwin
Various cast members
Nelson Riddle (d. 1985)

Producer:
Voyle Gilmore

1   That Terrific Rainbow (1:43)
2   I Didn't Know What Time It Was (2:46)
3   Do It The Hard Way (1:55)
4   Great Big Town (1:05)
5   There's A Small Hotel (2:33)
6   Zip (3:03)
7   I Could Write A Book (3:52)
8   Bewitched (4:26)
9   The Lady Is A Tramp (3:13)
10 Plant You Now, Dig You Later (1:46)
11 My Funny Valentine (2:01)
12 You Mustn't Kick It Around (1:38)
13 Bewitched (3:38)
14 Strip Number (3:24)
15 Dream Sequence & Finale: What Do I Care For A Dame, Bewitched, I Could Write A Book (6:01)

Total album length: 43 minutes

Frank Sinatra

SM-912

from the soundtrack
of the Columbia Picture

Rodgers and Hart's

PAL JOEY

An Essex-George Sidney Production

83 A Swingin' Affair

• **Album sales:** Under 500,000 | • **Highest position:** 2 (1 week) | • **Release date:** 1957

Frank Sinatra's career was firmly into its second phase by the time he recorded *A Swingin' Affair* in early 1957. Capitol Records was now presenting him as an albums artist, and he went on to make a top-selling series of recordings in the 1950s with arranger Nelson Riddle, his long-time musical collaborator.

A Swingin' Affair was deliberately conceived as a sequel to the previous year's enormously popular *Songs For Swingin' Lovers*. However, the musical approach was somewhat different. On this follow-up album, more brass instrumentation was used in the arrangements, with the result that the overall sound is a great deal more brash. Sinatra also sings with more attack. The songs, for the most part, were tried-and-tested classics

by the likes of Cole Porter, George Gershwin, and Duke Ellington. The opening 'Night and Day' was a song that Sinatra had first recorded over a decade earlier. Other classics included 'Nice Work If You Can Get It' and 'At Long Last Love'.

Despite its follow-up potential, *A Swingin' Affair* didn't quite match the success of the previous album, *Songs For Swingin' Lovers*. However, it reached Number Two in the charts, and stayed on the list for 36 weeks.

Number One singles:
None

Grammy awards:
None

Label: US: Capitol

Recorded in: Hollywood, USA

Personnel:
Frank Sinatra (d. 1998)
Nelson Riddle

Producer:
Voyle Gilmore

1   Night And Day (3:58)
2   I Wish I Were In Love Again (2:27)
3   I Got Plenty O' Nuttin' (3:09)
4   I Guess I'll Have To Change My Plan (2:23)
5   Nice Work If You Can Get It (2:20)
6   Stars Fell On Alabama (2:37)
7   No One Ever Tells You (3:23)
8   I Won't Dance (3:21)
9   Lonesome Road (3:53)
10 At Long Last Love (2:23)
11 You'd Be So Nice To Come Home To (2:03)
12 I Got It Bad And That Ain't Good (3:21)
13 From This Moment On (3:50)
14 If I Had You (2:35)
15 Oh! Look At Me Now (2:48)

Total album length: 48 minutes

Frank Sinatra

FRANK SINATRA
Capitol RECORDS
CAPITOL RECORDS HIGH FIDELITY RECORDING
a Swingin' Affair!

Star Dust

| • **Album sales:** Under 500,000 | • **Highest position:** 2 (1 week) | • **Release date:** 1958 |

By the summer of 1958, when *Star Dust* was released, Pat Boone was arguably the biggest pop star in America, having just been voted the favourite male singer of 1957 – ahead, even, of Elvis Presley. Boone's supremely smooth reading of rock 'n' roll hits (mostly covers of songs by black artists such as Little Richard and Fats Domino) were by now dominating the singles charts: his last seven singles had all been million sellers. However, like most teen-oriented acts of the day, he had not had a big hit album.

Star Dust was explicitly designed to change all that. This was almost entirely a ballad collection – the only exceptions being 'Little White Lies' and 'St. Louis Blues'. Boone's performance here made it very clear that he was, at heart, a crooner. The songs chosen were mostly popular standards, from Hoagy Carmichael's title track to Kurt Weill's closing 'September Song', though the mix is spiced up a little by his takes on 'Blueberry Hill' and Hank Williams' 'Cold, Cold Heart'. Certainly it was a mix that succeeded in broadening Boone's audience and it became a bestselling release, reaching Number Two in the charts during a total stay of 32 weeks.

Number One singles:
None

Grammy awards:
None

Label: US: Dot

Recorded in: Hollywood, USA

Personnel:
Pat Boone
Billy Vaughn (d. 1991)

Producer: N/A

1 **Star Dust** (3:17)
2 **Blueberry Hill** (2:23)
3 **Ebb Tide** (2:44)
4 **Little White Lies** (2:01)
5 **To Each His Own** (2:37)
6 **Cold, Cold Heart** (2:11)
7 **Deep Purple** (2:52)
8 **Autumn Leaves** (3:00)
9 **St. Louis Blues** (2:31)
10 **Solitude** (2:58)
11 **Anniversary Song** (3:16)
12 **Heartaches** (2:12)
13 **I'll Walk Alone** (1:57)
14 **September Song** (3:03)

Total album length: 37 minutes

Pat Boone

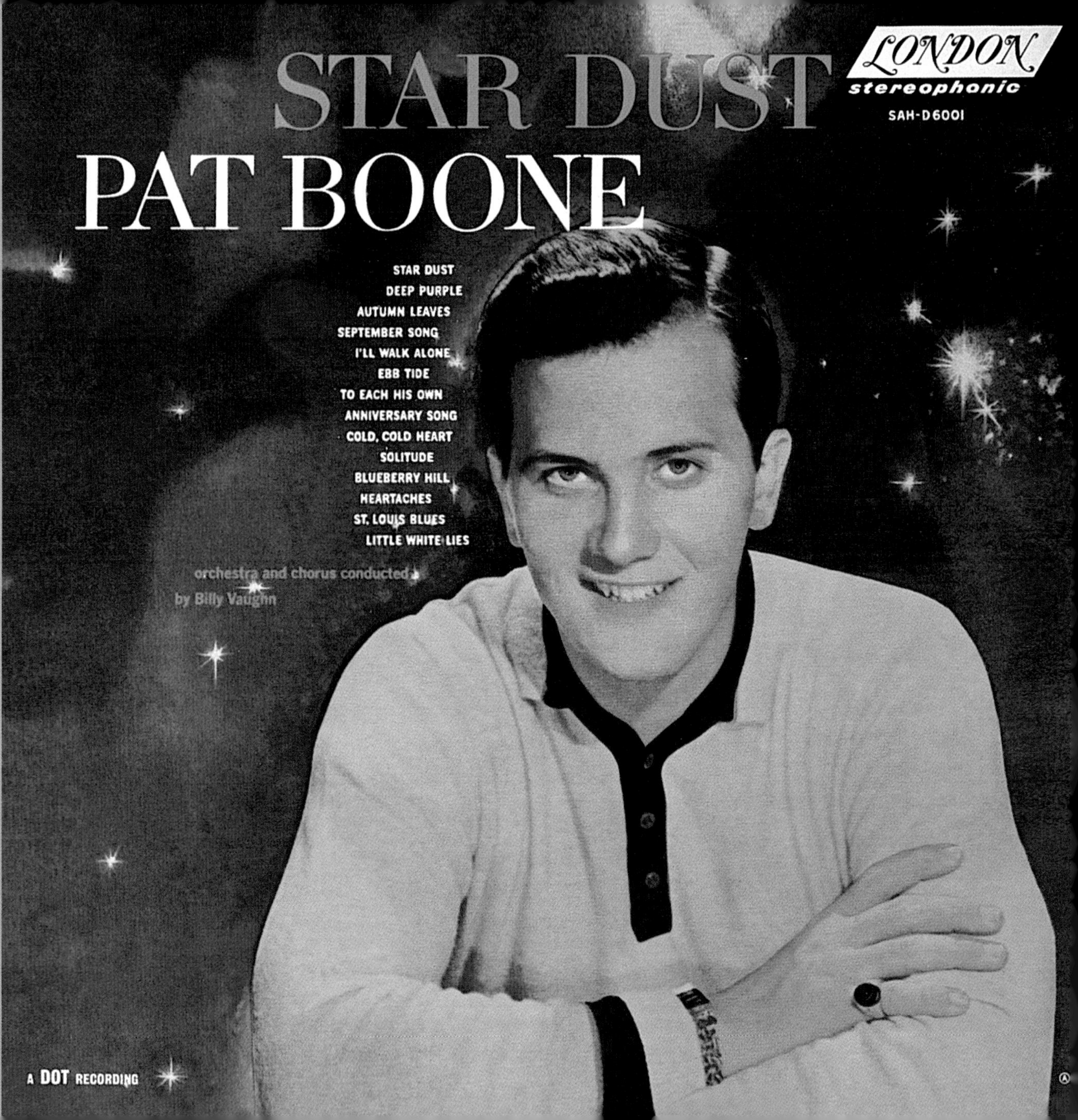

STAR DUST

PAT BOONE

LONDON
stereophonic
SAH-D 6001

STAR DUST
DEEP PURPLE
AUTUMN LEAVES
SEPTEMBER SONG
I'LL WALK ALONE
EBB TIDE
TO EACH HIS OWN
ANNIVERSARY SONG
COLD, COLD HEART
SOLITUDE
BLUEBERRY HILL
HEARTACHES
ST. LOUIS BLUES
LITTLE WHITE LIES

orchestra and chorus conducted
by Billy Vaughn

A DOT RECORDING

81 Romantic Jazz

| • **Album sales:** Under 500,000 | • **Highest position:** 2 (2 weeks) | • **Release date:** 1954 |

In 1954, when he recorded *Romantic Jazz*, Jackie Gleason (now best remembered for his part as Minnesota Fats in *The Hustler*), was one of the biggest names in American TV, the star of the hit show *The Honeymooners*. The year before, he had proposed to Capitol Records that he record an album of romantic mood music for the label. The album went on to become a big surprise hit. Gleason, a virtual non-musician, had stumbled upon a hot formula.

The formula was a simple matter of getting an orchestra to play romantic standards; but, rather than emphasizing their skills, the orchestra was required to underplay. Gleason himself did not appear on the albums, but had an important role as producer. *Romantic Jazz* was the fourth full album in the series and it saw Gleason plus his

regular arranger Pete King and lead trumpet player Bobby Hackett working their way through a relatively uptempo set, including the likes of 'Crazy Rhythm' and 'The Lady Is A Tramp'.

Released just before Billboard started their album chart, *Romantic Jazz* finally charted in late 1955, following the huge success of Gleason's *Lonesome Echo* album. It reached Number Two during a stay of 11 weeks.

Number One singles:
None

Grammy awards:
None

Label: US: Capitol

Recorded in: N/A

Personnel:
Pete King
Bobby Hackett

Producer:
Jackie Gleason (d. 1987)

1　There'll Be Some Changes Made (3:06)
2　How About You? (3:01)
3　Crazy Rhythm (3:12)
4　The Petite Waltz (3:12)
5　Don't Blame Me (3:16)
6　You Can't Pull The Wool Over My Eyes (2:52)
7　Soon (3:12)
8　My Blue Heaven (3:15)
9　The Lady Is A Tramp (3:28)
10　The Most Beautiful Girl In The World (3:02)
11　Who Cares (3:17)
12　I've Got My Eyes On You (2:50)
13　The Best Things In Life Are Free (2:34)
14　I Never Knew (3:14)
15　The World Is Waiting For The Sunrise (2:22)
16　The Love Nest (3:34)

Total album length: 49 minutes

JACKIE GLEASON
plays ROMANTIC JAZZ

I've Got My Eyes On You • Soon • The Petite Waltz

The World Is Waiting For The Sunrise • The Love Nest • The Lady Is A Tramp

How About You? • There'll Be Some Changes Made • Crazy Rhythm • Don't Blame Me

The Best Things In Life Are Free • My Blue Heaven • I Never Knew • Who Cares?

The Most Beautiful Girl In The World • You Can't Pull The Wool Over My Eyes

80 King Creole

| • **Album sales:** Under 500,000 | • **Highest position:** 2 (2 weeks) | • **Release date:** October 1958 |

Elvis' first original album of 1958, following on from the greatest hits collection *Elvis' Golden Records*, was another movie tie-in. This time it included all 11 songs that Elvis had sung in the New Orleans-set movie *King Creole*. Both the film and album were made in the knowledge that, as soon as they were completed, Elvis was to go into the army. It would be two years till he recorded again, so *King Creole* represents the end of the first phase of Elvis Presley's career.

The album was recorded as usual in Hollywood with his regular band, though this time they were augmented by the Paramount Studio Orchestra. The arrangements were more elaborate throughout. Obvious standouts include the title track, 'King Creole', written by the album's effective producers Leiber and Stoller, the ballad 'As Long As I Have You', and a rocker, 'Hard Headed Woman', which gave Elvis yet another Number One single.

It should be noted that in its original form the album barely lasted 20 minutes. This may explain why *King Creole* was Elvis' first original album release to fail to make Number One or to be certified gold. It peaked at Number Two but was denied the top slot by Mitch Miller.

Number One singles:
US: Hard Headed Woman

Grammy awards:
None

Label: US & UK: RCA

Recorded: Hollywood, USA

Personnel:
Elvis Presley (d. 1977)
Scotty Moore
Bill Black
D.J. Fontana
Dudley Brooks
The Jordanaires
Paramount Studio
  Orchestra

Producers :
Jerry Leiber
Mike Stoller (uncredited)

1   **King Creole** (2:12)
2   **As Long As I Have You** (1:53)
3   **Hard Headed Woman** (1:57)
4   **Trouble** (2:21)
5   **Dixieland Rock** (1:50)
6   **Don`t Ask Me Why** (2:10)
7   **Lover Doll** (2:13)
8   **Crawfish** (1:53)
9   **Young Dreams** (2:26)
10 **Steadfast, Loyal And True** (1:19)
11 **New Orleans** (1:59)

Total album length: 22 minutes

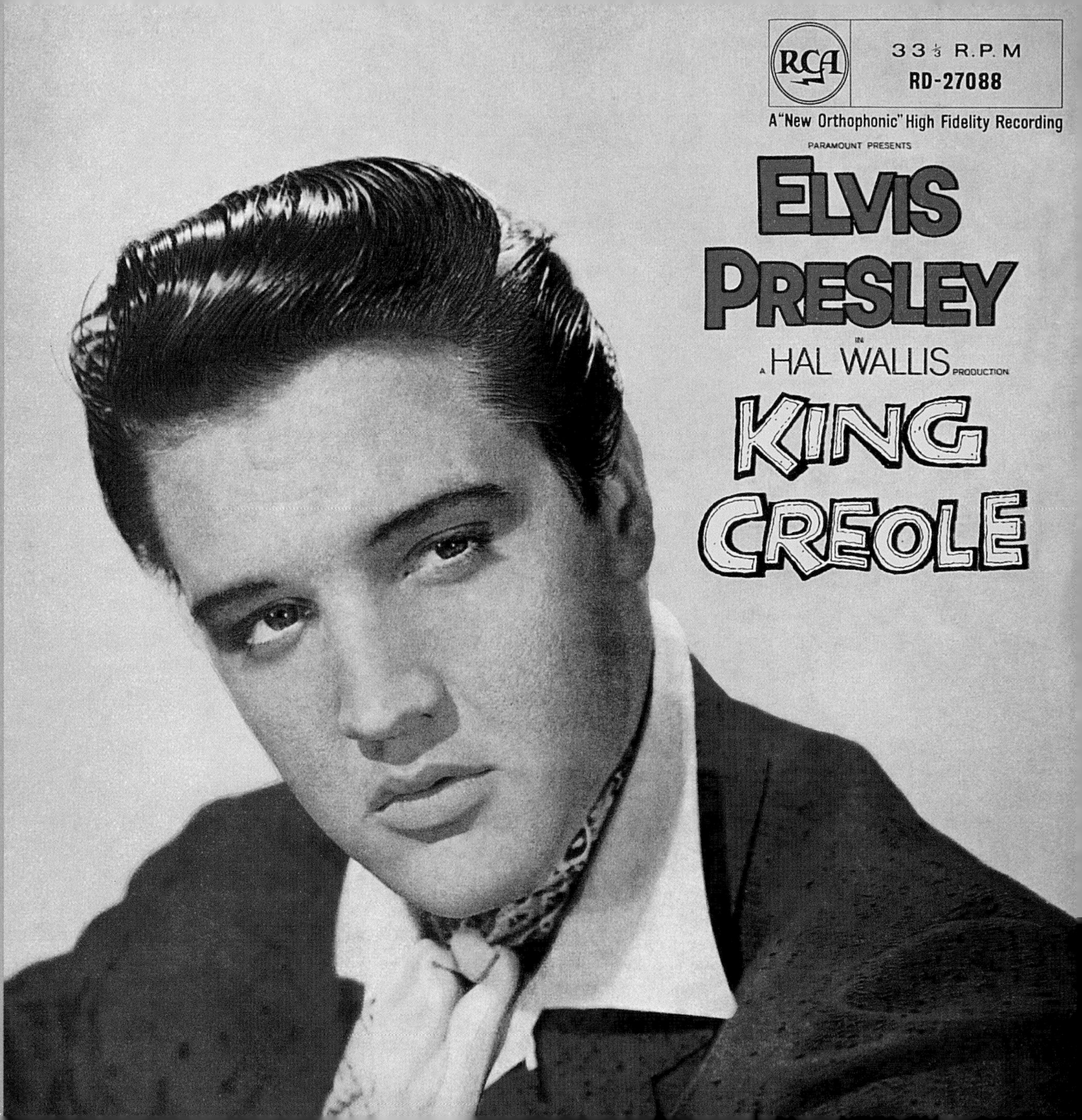

33⅓ R.P.M
RD-27088

A "New Orthophonic" High Fidelity Recording

PARAMOUNT PRESENTS

ELVIS PRESLEY

IN A HAL WALLIS PRODUCTION

KING CREOLE

No One Cares

| • **Album sales:** Under 500,000 | • **Highest position:** 2 (2 weeks) | • **Release date:** 1959 |

*N*o One Cares was Sinatra's second album of 1959, following on from the Grammy award-winning *Come Dance With Me*. As that album was most definitely a swinging affair, it was inevitable that the follow-up would be a ballad collection. As the title suggests, this is Sinatra at his most determinedly lovelorn. The cover says it all, showing him standing alone at a bar while happy lovers dance around him (no doubt to the strains of *Come Dance With Me*).

In effect *No One Cares* is a companion piece to the 1957 ballad collection *Where Were You*: they share the same arranger, Gordon Jenkins, and the same lush yet melancholy string arrangements. It's a record that positively wallows in loneliness. As ever, the title cut comes from Sinatra's favourite writing team of Cahn & Van Heusen. Other classic tracks include 'Stormy Weather' and 'I Don't Stand A Ghost Of A Chance With You', creating an album that had critics comparing Sinatra to Billie Holiday in the sophisticated sorrow stakes.

No One Cares wasn't quite as successful as *Come Dance With Me*, but still made Number Two in the charts and remained there for 30 weeks, just catching the new decade.

Number One singles:
None

Grammy awards:
None

Label: US & UK: Capitol

Recorded in: Hollywood, USA

Personnel:
Frank Sinatra (d. 1998)
Gordon Jenkins (d. 1984)

Producer:
Dave Cavanaugh

1　**When No One Cares**　(2:42)
2　**Cottage For Sale**　(3:16)
3　**Stormy Weather**　(3:20)
4　**Where Do You Go?**　(2:34)
5　**I Don't Stand A Ghost Of A Chance With You**　(3:16)
6　**Here's That Rainy Day**　(3:34)
7　**I Can't Get Started**　(4:01)
8　**Why Try To Change Me Now?**　(3:41)
9　**Just Friends**　(3:40)
10　**I'll Never Smile Again**　(3:46)
11　**None But The Lonely Heart**　(3:41)

Total album length: 43 minutes

Frank Sinatra

no one cares / **FRANK SINATRA**

ORCHESTRA CONDUCTED BY GORDON JENKINS

78 The Man With The Golden Arm

• **Album sales:** Under 500,000 | • **Highest position:** 2 (4 weeks) | • **Release date:** 1956

On its release, *The Man With The Golden Arm* shocked movie audiences with its honest depiction of heroin addiction. Based on a novel by Nelson Algren, the character of Frankie Machine, a jazz drummer struggling to stay off heroin, was played by Frank Sinatra. The film also starred Kim Novak as his long-suffering mistress, and Eleanor Parker as his hysterical wife. One of the highlights of this ground-breaking film, directed by Otto Preminger, was the jazz soundtrack.

Preminger took a chance on hiring composer Elmer Bernstein to write the score, which was later nominated for an Oscar. Deeply influenced by modern jazz, Bernstein's approach was innovative. The structure of the music was unusual, its dynamics making reference to the influence of the be-bop movement, albeit in a mainstream idiom. Working with Bernstein on the arrangements was trumpeter and bandleader Shorty Rogers, who was also to become known for bringing modern jazz into movie soundtracks.

Not only did the subject matter of the film arouse controversy, Bernstein's soundtrack also created a stir. The album release sold well, not only to jazz aficionados, but also to general film goers, It reached Number Two on the Billboard album charts in 1956.

Number One singles:
None

Grammy awards:
None

Label: US: Decca

Recorded in: N/A

Personnel:
Elmer Bernstein
Shorty Rogers
Shelly Manne
Pete Candoli
Bob Cooper
Bud Shank
Ray Turner
Milt Bernhart

Producers: N/A

1 Clarke Street (5:00)
2 Zosh (4:30)
3 Frankie Machine (4:59)
4 The Fix (3:32)
5 Molly (4:58)
6 Breakup (3:45)
7 Sunday Morning (2:51)
8 Desperation (2:50)
9 Audition (2:45)
10 The Cure (5:59)
11 Finale (4:13)

Total album length: 45 minutes

Music from the Sound Track...

DECCA RECORDS

music by Elmer Bernstein from "The Man With The Golden Arm"

THE MAN WITH THE GOLDEN ARM

A FILM BY OTTO PREMINGER

Sleeve design by Saul Bass

DESIGNED BY SAUL BASS

jazz sequences arranged and played by SHORTY ROGERS and His Giants with SHELLY MANNE
courtesy Atlantic Records   courtesy Contemporary Records

DL 8257

Printed in U.S.A.

In The Wee Small Hours

| • **Album sales:** Under 500,000 | • **Highest position:** 2 (18 weeks) | • **Release date:** 1955 |

This was Sinatra's first 12-inch album for Capitol Records, the label that rescued his career after Mitch Miller had dropped him from the Columbia roster. The 10-inch mini-album that preceded it, *Songs For Young Lovers*, had seen Sinatra dabbling with the notion of a set of thematically linked songs, but the longer 12-inch format allowed him to do the concept full justice.

With Capitol's top arranger Nelson Riddle at his side, Sinatra set out to create a mood of pure melancholy. Even the sleeve picked up the theme with its portrait of Sinatra alone on a darkened street, smoking a cigarette. The songs were a collection of certified classics, from the newly written title track to Rodgers and Hart's 'It Never Entered My Mind'. The album was reputedly inspired by the break-up of Sinatra's love affair with Ava Gardner; whatever the truth, critics agreed that he had never sounded more heartbroken. There was also a significantly jazzier touch than on much of Sinatra's later work, partly inspired by Bill Miller's piano playing.

In The Wee Small Hours was an early entry into Billboard's brand new albums chart. It peaked at Number Two and remained on the charts for 33 weeks.

Number One singles:
None

Grammy awards:
None

Label: Capitol

Recorded in: Hollywood, USA

Personnel:
Frank Sinatra (d. 1998)
Nelson Riddle

Producer:
Voyle Gilmore

1   In the Wee Small Hours Of The Morning (3:00)
2   Mood Indigo (3:30)
3   Glad To Be Unhappy (2:35)
4   I Get Along Without You Very Well (3:42)
5   Deep In A Dream (2:49)
6   I See Your Face Before Me (3:24)
7   Can't We Be Friends? (2:48)
8   When Your Lover Has Gone (3:10)
9   What Is This Thing Called Love (2:35)
10 Last Night When We Were Young (3:17)
11 I'll Be Around (2:59)
12 Ill Wind (3:46)
13 It Never Entered My Mind (2:42)
14 Dancing On The Ceiling (2:57)
15 I'll Never Be The Same (3:05)
16 This Love Of Mine (3:33)

Total album length: 49 minutes

FRANK SINATRA

in the **wee small hours**

76 The Eddie Duchin Story

| • **Album sales:** Under 500,000 | • **Highest position:** 1 (1 week) | • **Release date:** 1956 |

This biographical movie about the pianist and orchestra leader Eddy Duchin starred Tyrone Power, Kim Novak, Victoria Shaw and James Whitmore. It told the story of pianist and bandleader Eddy Duchin, who had thrilled nightclub audiences in the 1930s with his spectacular piano playing, which included tricks like reversing hands in the middle of a piece. 'Ten Magic Fingers', as Duchin was known, appeared to lead a charmed life until the death of his wife Marjorie in childbirth.

The film, directed by George Sidney, was a classic Hollywood weepie, albeit of a high-class variety. For many critics, its best feature was the soundtrack, played off screen by Carmen Cavallaro. Power, who took the role of Duchin, had to train intensively to mimic the pianist's style. Highlights of the soundtrack include 'To Love Again' (based on Chopin's E-Flat Nocturne) and 'Manhattan'. In the film, Power (dubbed by Cavallaro) also plays an entertaining version of 'Chopsticks' with a Filipino urchin boy, which helps lead him out of depression, and prompts him to take an interest in his young son.

The soundtrack was released in 1956 and reached the Number One on the Billboard charts, remaining there for a total of 99 weeks.

Number One singles: None	**Recorded in:** N/A
Grammy awards: None	**Personnel:** Carmen Cavallaro (d. 1989)
Label: US: Decca	**Producers:** N/A

1 To Love Again
2 Manhattan
3 Shine On Harvest Moon
4 It Must Be True
5 Whispering
6 Dizzy Fingers
7 You´re My Everything
8 Chopsticks
9 On The Sunny Side Of The Street
10 Brazil
11 La Vie En Rose
12 To Love Again

Total album length: 34 minutes

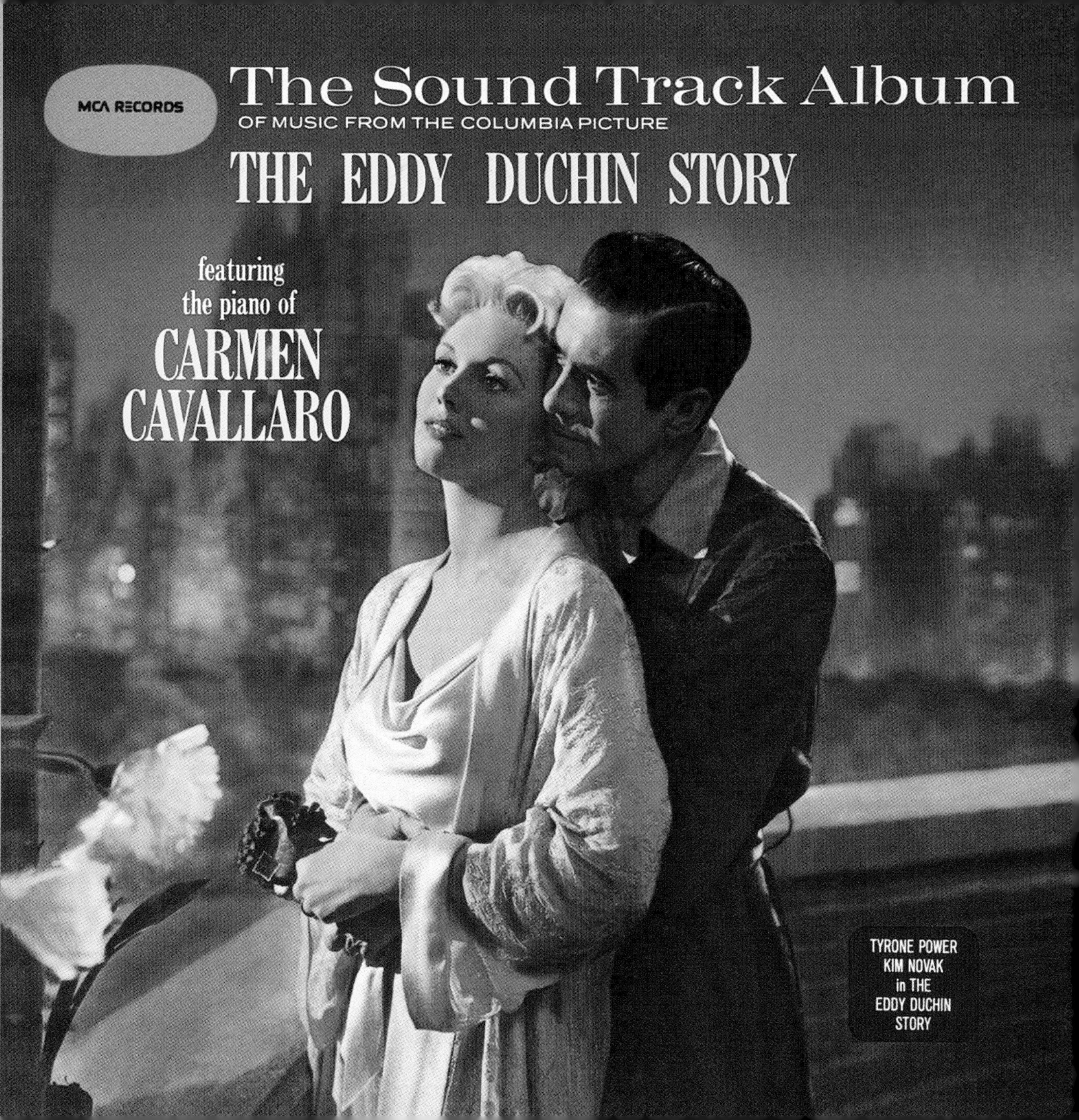
MCA RECORDS
The Sound Track Album
OF MUSIC FROM THE COLUMBIA PICTURE
THE EDDY DUCHIN STORY
featuring the piano of
CARMEN CAVALLARO
TYRONE POWER
KIM NOVAK
in THE
EDDY DUCHIN
STORY

75 Crazy Otto

• **Album sales:** Under 500,000 | • **Highest position:** 1 (2 weeks) | • **Release date:** April 1955

Even by the standards of the 1950s, when novelty hits were not uncommon, the success of Crazy Otto's first album was extraordinary. Crazy Otto was the pseudonym of Fritz Schulz-Reichel, a German jazz musician who had been a popular entertainer in Europe before and after World War II. Schulz-Reichel specialized in a kind of piano-based comedy not unlike that of Victor Borge, but based around popular rather than classical music. In 1953 he'd taken on the Crazy Otto persona, which saw him backed by a small jazz combo, including German jazz guitarist Ladi Geisler.

Otto recorded the eponymous *Crazy Otto* album for Deutsche Grammophon in Germany, but its success quickly spread across the Atlantic and in 1955 it was released in the USA by Decca. It caught on very fast. There was nothing subtle about Otto's music – he simply performed straighforward honky-tonk or rag-time interpretations of familiar tunes, laced with humour thanks to his unique invention, 'the Tipsy Wire Box', a device that made any piano, no matter how grand, sound like an out-of-tune, honky-tonk bar-room piano.

Crazy Otto's debut album made it all the way to Number One, where it stayed for two weeks in the spring of 1955.

Number One singles:
None

Grammy awards:
None

Label: US: Decca

Recorded in: Germany

Personnel:
Crazy Otto (Fritz
    Schulz-Reichel)
Ladi Geisler

Producer: N/A

1 Glad Rag Doll
2 Beautiful Ohio
3 My Melancholy Baby
4 Red Sails In The Sunset
5 In The Mood
6 Smiles
7 Rose Of Washington Square
8 S-h-i-n-e
9 Paddlin' Madelin' Home
10 Lights Out

Official times not available

Crazy Otto

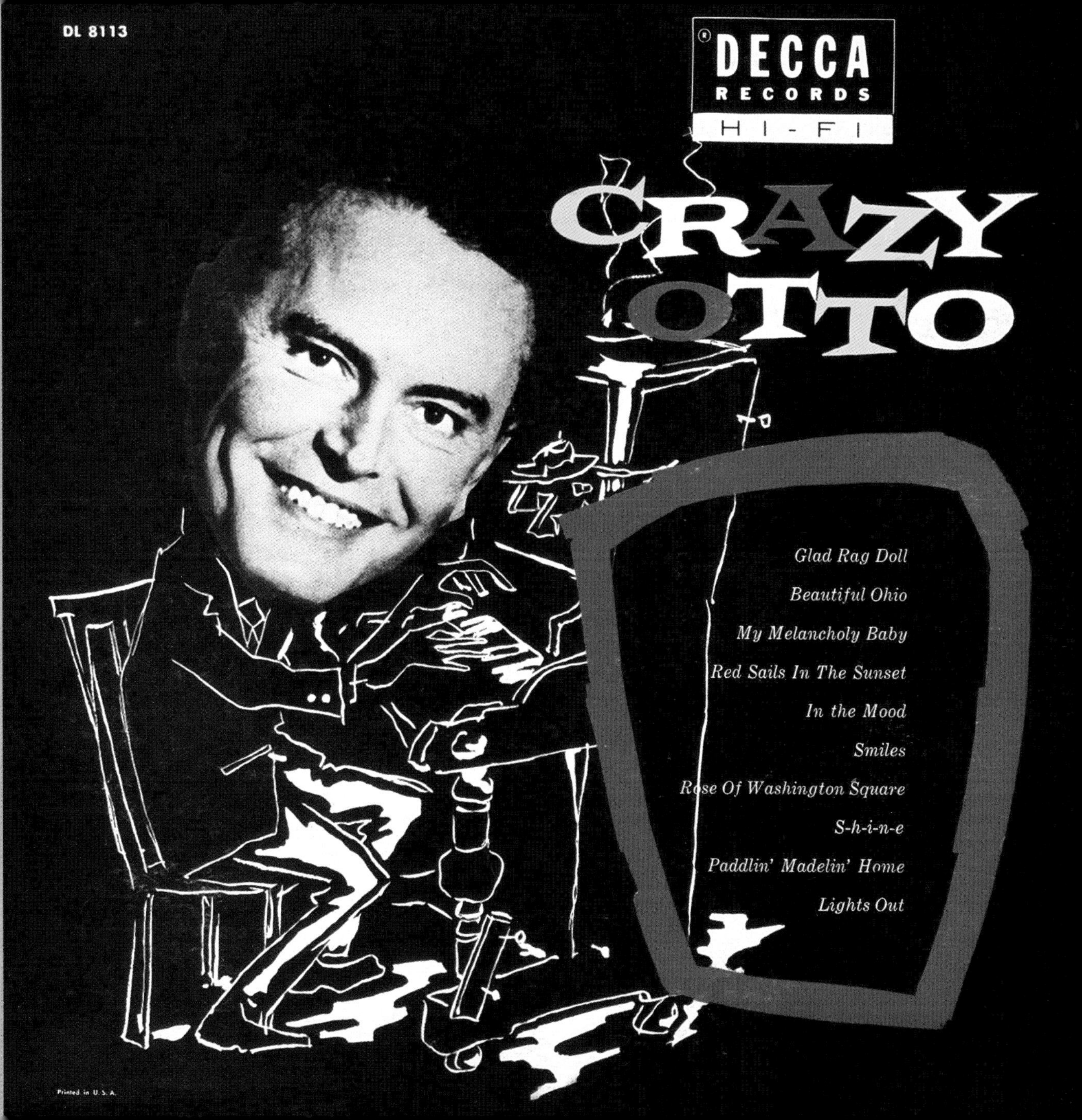

DL 8113

DECCA
RECORDS
HI-FI

CRAZY OTTO

Glad Rag Doll

Beautiful Ohio

My Melancholy Baby

Red Sails In The Sunset

In the Mood

Smiles

Rose Of Washington Square

S-h-i-n-e

Paddlin' Madelin' Home

Lights Out

Printed in U.S.A.

74 Lonesome Echo

• **Album sales:** Under 500,000 | • **Highest position:** 1 (2 weeks) | • **Release date:** 1955

Despite the fact that the actor Jackie Gleason was scarcely a musician at all, his series of mood music albums were in some ways more sophisticated than their nearest rivals during the 1950s, which were the easy listening orchestrations of Mantovani and his orchestra. Gleason's sophistication was conceptual as much as musical. He understood that the function of easy listening music was to create a mood, not to distract the listener with complex, intricate, or over-dramatic arrangements.

The sleeve was specially designed by the great surrealist painter, Salvador Dali (a feature that has made the album a desirable collectible ever since). The record itself follows Gleason's formula for romantic listening: an orchestra plays softly, while the great trumpeter and cornettist

Bobby Hackett plays a distant melody. The songs Gleason chose this time around – from 'Speak Low' to 'The Thrill Is Gone' – have a slightly more reflective, melancholy feel than on his other albums, but as ever it is the general mood that dominates, rather than the tracks.

Lonesome Echo was Gleason's first album to make the Number One spot – it spent two weeks there during a 22-week stay on the charts.

Number One singles:
None

Grammy awards:
None

Label: US: Capitol

Recorded in: N/A

Personnel:
Pete King
Bobby Hackett

Producer:
Jackie Gleason (d. 1987)

1   **There Must Be A Way** (2:58)
2   **Mad About The Boy** (3:18)
3   **Come Rain Or Come Shine** (3:15)
4   **Deep Purple** (3:20)
5   **Someday I'll Find You** (2:38)
6   **The Thrill Is Gone** (3:15)
7   **How Deep Is The Ocean** (3:34)
8   **Speak Low** (3:45)
9   **Garden In The Rain** (3:21)
10 **Remember** (2:42)
11 **I Still Get A Thrill** (3:07)
12 **Dancing On The Ceiling** (2:53)

Total album length: 38 minutes

Jackie Gleason presents

LONESOME ECHO

collectors' choice® MUSIC

Sleeve artwork by Salvador Dali

73 Ricky

• **Album sales:** Under 500,000 │ • **Highest position:** 1 (2 weeks) │ • **Release date:** October 1957 │

Ricky Nelson's debut album was one of the very few rock'n'roll albums to become a major hit – this was a market dominated by singles. However, Nelson had more than a few advantages when it came to selling records.

Nelson was a weekly fixture on TV, playing himself in the enormously popular 'Ozzy & Harriett' Show (a sitcom based on his real-life family). The American public had seen Ricky Nelson grow from wisecracking kid to teenage heartthrob and, when he turned to singing, he was an immediate smash, with his records featured heavily in the show.

Perhaps surprisingly, Ricky Nelson went on to become more than a novelty act. He had a genuine love for the new music, a crack band featuring future Elvis sideman James Burton, and an ear for a good song. The first single from the album, 'Be-Bop Baby', was an effectively restrained slice of pop rockabilly. Throw in a couple of covers of songs from rougher-edged rockers like Carl Perkins and Jerry Lee Lewis, plus a clutch of ballads for the older folks, and the result was an album that made rock'n'roll palatable but not bland. Ricky went straight to Number One and spent two weeks there.

Number One singles:
None

Grammy awards:
None

Label: US: Imperial

Recorded in: Los Angeles, USA

Personnel:
Ricky Nelson (d. 1985)
James Burton
Joe Maphis
James Kirkland
Richie Frost

Producer: N/A

1 Honeycomb (2:54)
2 Boppin' The Blues (1:56)
3 Be-Bop Baby (2:01)
4 Have I Told You Lately That I Love You (1:58)
5 Teenage Doll (1:48)
6 If You Can't Rock Me (1:53)
7 Whole Lotta Shakin' Goin' On (2:11)
8 Baby I'm Sorry (2:21)
9 Am I Blue (1:39)
10 I'm Confessin' (2:16)
11 Your True Love (1:58)
12 True Love (2:17)

Total album length: 24 minutes

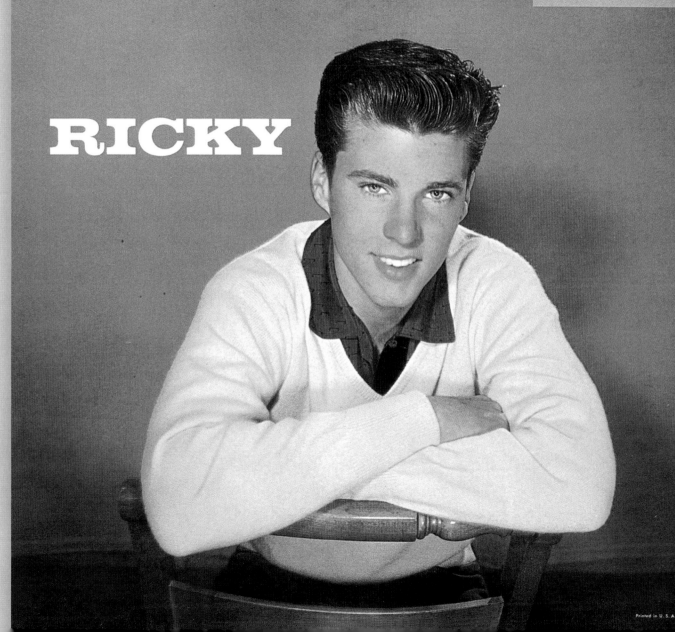

RICKY

I-R
IMPERIAL LP 9048
HI-FIDELITY

Printed in U. S. A.

72 Come Fly With Me

• **Album sales:** Under 500,000 │ • **Highest position:** 1 (5 weeks) │ • **Release date:** 1958

One of the best loved of all Sinatra's classic Capitol albums, *Come Fly With Me* was the first of his uptempo albums to be recorded without the aid of master arranger Nelson Riddle. In place of Riddle, Sinatra hooked up with Billy May, a former Glenn Miller arranger who had led a Capitol studio big band through the early 1950s.

May's arrangements brought a brash, brassy confidence to the album; this was the sound of Sinatra kicking back and having fun. It's nicely set up by the specially commissioned Cahn/Van Heusen title track and from then on Sinatra takes the listener on a musical whistle stop tour of the world – from the 'Isle Of Capri' via 'April In Paris' and 'London By Night' to 'Blue Hawaii'. As the closing number points out 'It's Nice To Go

Trav'ling, and so it is, on what is not just one of Sinatra's most light-hearted records but also one of his most varied.

The public were happy to go along for the ride too, and *Come Fly With Me* became Sinatra's first ever Number One album. It remained at the top for five weeks and on the charts for some 50 weeks. Billy May would return again to arrange 1959's *Come Dance With Me* and 1961's *Come Swing With Me* but though these later works may have swung more broadly (especially the 1959 release), they never fully recaptured the carefree joy of this initial collaboration.

Number One singles:
None

Grammy awards:
None

Label: US: Capitol

Recorded in:
Hollywood, USA

Personnel:
Frank Sinatra (d. 1998)
Billy May

Producer:
Voyle Gilmore

1 **Come Fly With Me** (3:19)
2 **Around The World** (3:20)
3 **Isle Of Capri** (2:29)
4 **Moonlight In Vermont** (3:32)
5 **Autumn In New York** (4:37)
6 **On The Road To Mandalay** (3:28)
7 **Let's Get Away From It All** (2:11)
8 **April In Paris** (2:50)
9 **London By Night** (3:30)
10 **Brazil** (2:55)
11 **Blue Hawaii** (2:44)
12 **It's Nice To Go Trav'ling** (3:52)

Total album length: 39 minutes

Frank Sinatra

SM-920
Capitol ®

Come fly with me

FRANK SINATRA

with **BILLY MAY** and his orchestra

71 Exotica

| • **Album sales:** Under 500,000 | • **Highest position:** 1 (5 weeks) | • **Release date:** 1959 |

For Martin Denny's *Exotica* album it was a case of second time lucky. Hawaiian bandleader Denny originally recorded *Exotica* in 1956 in what Liberty Records described grandly as 'Spectra-Sonic' Mono. It failed to reach the charts. However, in 1958 a vogue for Hawaiian music swept America, and Liberty decided to revive the album. So they sent Denny back into the studio to re-record the album in stereo.

This was a smart move. Denny's instrumental sound was full of odd sound effects such as imitation bird calls and the new stereo technology showed it off to full advantage. Sure enough, second time around the album made it all the way to the Number One spot, where it remained for five weeks, aided no doubt by its lavish sleeve featuring the model Sandy Warner ('the Exotica girl'). The album's hit single 'Quiet Village', which reached Number Two in the Billboard singles charts.

Martin Denny's sound was based around a quartet featuring himself on piano, Arthur Lyman on vibes (replaced by Julius Wechter for the stereo version), Augie Colon on percussion (and bird calls) and John Kramer on bass. Their material (including the single 'Quiet Village') was largely taken from the oeuvre of exotic lounge music king Les Baxter.

Martin Denny

Number One singles:
None

Grammy awards:
None

Label: US: Liberty

Recorded in:
Los Angeles, USA

Personnel:
Martin Denny
Julius Wechter
Augie Colon
John Kramer
Harvey Ragsdale

Producers:
Si Waronker

1   Quiet Village (3:39)
2   Return To Paradise (2:19)
3   Hong Kong Blues (2:15)
4   Busy Port (2:50)
5   Lotus Land (2:22)
6   Similau (1:57)
7   Stone God (3:07)
8   Jungle Flower (1:46)
9   China Nights (2:01)
10 Ah Me Furi (2:08)
11 Waipo (3:11)
12 Love Dance (2:29)

Total album length: 29 minutes

THE SOUNDS OF **Martin Denny**

EXOTICA

PRINTED IN U.S.A.

SPECTRA-SONIC-SOUND   *the ultimate in hi-fidelity*

LRP 3034

70 Starring Sammy Davis Jr.

• Album sales: Under 500,000 │ **• Highest position:** 1 (6 weeks) │ **• Release date:** April 1955 │

1954 had been a pivotal year in the career of Sammy Davis Jr. After 25 years treading the boards he'd made it to the top of the cabaret world. He'd been the first black entertainer to play New York's Copacabana – helped by his friend Frank Sinatra – and now he was the first black act to play one of the main rooms in Las Vegas. He was a regular on the *Colgate Comedy Hour*, and he had a brand new recording contract with Decca.

Then, driving from Las Vegas to Los Angeles to record the theme for a new film, Davis had a terrible car accident, resulting in the loss of one eye. Rather than ending his career, however, his accident resulted in a vast national outpouring of sympathy. Decca decided to capitalize on this by releasing his first ever album. *Starring Sammy Davis Jr.* was a mixture of material recorded before and after the crash. Its release was preceded by a single, 'Birth Of The Blues', that gained added resonance from Davis' accident, as did other cuts such as 'Lonesome Road' and 'Stan' Up An' Fight'.

Buoyed by the sympathy vote, Davis' album was an immediate Number One hit, staying at the top for six weeks.

Number One singles:
None

Grammy awards:
None

Label: US: Decca;
UK: Brunswick

Recorded in: New York and Los Angeles, USA

Personnel:
Sammy Davis Jr. (d. 1990)
Sy Oliver Orchestra
Morty Stevens' Orchestra

Producer: N/A

1 Lonesome Road
2 Hey There
3 And This Is My Beloved
4 September Song
5 Easy To Love
6 Glad To Be Unhappy
7 Stan' Up An' Fight
8 My Funny Valentine
9 Spoken For
10 The Birth Of The Blues

Official times not available

Starring Sammy Davis Jr.

LONG 33⅓ RPM PLAYING

Brunswick RECORDS

LAT 8153

69 Tchaikovsky: Piano Concerto No.1

| • **Album sales:** Under 500,000 | • **Highest position:** 1 (7 weeks) | • **Release date:** 1958 |

Not just a remarkable recording of a classic concerto, Van Cliburn's recording of Tchaikovsky's First is a piece of history in its own right. Van Cliburn was arguably the most celebrated classical performer of the modern era, renowned for his flawless technical prowess and unparalleled romantic sensibility.

In April 1958 Cliburn, a tall, good looking, young Texan, was the USA's representative at the First International Tchaikovsky Piano Competition, held in Moscow at the height of the Cold War. The former child prodigy Cliburn's performance was so sensational that the Russian audience began to chant, 'First prize, first prize'. The judges were initially frightened to give such a prestigious award to an American, but, having got clearance from Khrushchev himself, Van Cliburn was duly awarded the first prize.

On his return home Cliburn, was suddenly a national hero. He was given a ticker tape parade in New York, the only classical musician to receive such an honour. He gave a sold-out performance at Carnegie Hall to a rapturous reception, then went into the recording studio to record the piece for an RCA album.

The album went straight to Number One and remained there for seven weeks, becoming the only classical recording in many 1950s American households, while Cliburn became, for a while, a star on a par with any pop idol.

Number One singles:
None

Grammy awards:
Best classical performance – instrumentalist (with concerto scale accompaniment)

Label: US: RCA Victor

Recorded in: N/A

Personnel:
Van Cliburn
Kiril Kondrashin
Symphony Of The Air Orchestra

Producer:
John Pfeiffer

1　Concerto 1 – Allegro Non Troppo E Molto Maestoso (20:41)
2　Concerto 1 – Andantino Simplice　(7:01)
3　Concerto 1 – Allegro Con Fuoco　(6:44)

Total album length: 34 minutes

Van Cliburn

TCHAIKOVSKY CONCERTO No. 1
VAN CLIBURN
KIRIL KONDRASHIN, Conductor

RCA VICTOR
LM-2252
RED SEAL
A "New Orthophonic" High Fidelity Recording

© RCA Printed in U.S.A.

Sleeve artwork by N Rakhmanoc from Sovfoto

68 Around The World In 80 Days

• Album sales: Under 500,000 | **• Highest position:** 1 (10 weeks) | **• Release date:** April 1957

The soundtrack of this popular film was released in 1957 and hit the Number One spot on the Billboard charts. The film, starring David Niven, Cantinflas, Robert Newton, and Shirley MacLaine, and had been a big box-office success, but it was unusual for an instrumental soundtrack of this kind to sell so well.

The score was by Victor Young, a well-known musical figure in the film world. Young, who worked on over 300 Hollywood movies, brought his immense experience and expertise as a conductor, arranger, composer and violinist to the project, with outstanding results.

The story centred around a Victorian Englishman, Phileas Fogg, who bets his entire fortune that he could circumnavigate the globe in 80 days. He travels with his butler, Passepartout, and the pair have many comical adventures on their voyage. The story was based on a novel by Jules Verne. Much of the music, such as 'Entrance Of The Bull March', 'India Countryside' and 'The Pagoda Of Pillagi' had an exotic flavour, which Young tackled with his customary flair.

So popular was the soundtrack album that it remained on the Billboard chart for a staggering 88 weeks. Young received an Academy Award for his film score.

Number One singles:	Label: US: Decca;
None	UK: Brunswick
Grammy awards:	Personnel:
None	Victor Young
Recorded in: N/A	Producers: N/A

1 **Around The World (Part I)** (3:01)
2 **Passepartout** (3:21)
3 **Paris Arrival** (2:47)
4 **Sky Symphony** (4:30)
5 **Entrance Of The Bull March** (2:34)
7 **India Countryside** (3:53)
8 **Around The World (Part II)** (1:04)
9 **The Pagoda of Pillagi** (4:00)
10 **Temple Of Dawn** (2:15)
11 **Prairie Sail Girl** (1:47)
12 **Land Ho** (6:56)
13 **Epilogue** (6:22)

Total album length: 42 minutes

LONG 33⅓ RPM PLAYING

Brunswick RECORDS

LAT 8185

Michael Todd's

AROUND THE WORLD IN

80

DAYS

MUSIC BY VICTOR YOUNG

67 Gigi

• **Album sales:** Under 500,000 | • **Highest position:** 1 (10 weeks) | • **Release date:** June 1958

The musical film *Gigi*, starring Leslie Caron, Maurice Chevalier, Louis Jordan and Hermione Gingold, was the first big hit from the partnership of Alan Jay Lerner and Frederick Loewe since the hugely popular 'My Fair Lady'.

Based on the novel by Colette, the story of Gigi was that of a Parisian ingénue, who is trained as a courtesan and becomes an elegant, beautiful young woman. The musical yielded two hit songs, 'Thank Heaven For Little Girls', performed by Maurice Chevalier, and the witty 'I Remember It Well', sung as a duet by Hermione Gingold and Maurice Chevalier. Both numbers then became part of Chevalier's standard repertoire. The voice of Gigi, played on screen by Leslie Caron, was mostly dubbed by Betty Wand, although Caron did sing parts of 'The Night They Invented Champagne'.

Conducting the MGM Studio Orchestra was André Previn, who was widely acclaimed for his work on the soundtrack which won a Grammy Award for Best soundtrack. *Gigi* the album hit the Number One spot on Billboard's charts and then spent 78 weeks there during 1958.

Number One singles:	**Personnel:**
None	Maurice Chevalier
	(d. 1972)
Grammy awards:	Leslie Caron
Best soundtrack album,	Betty Wand
dramatic picture score or	Louis Jordan
original cast	Hermione Gingold
	John Abbott
Label: US: MGM	André Previn
Recorded in: N/A	**Producers:** N/A

1 Overture (Orchestra) (1:59)
2 Honore's Soliloquy (2:36)
3 Thank Heaven For Little Girls (2:43)
4 It's A Bore (3:19)
5 The Parisians (3:13)
6 The Waltz At The Ice Rink (2:24)
7 The Gossips (2:21)
8 She Is Not Thinking Of Me (2:26)
9 It's A Bore (0:55)
10 Gaston Celebrates (Orchestra) (2:17)
11 The Night They Invented Champagne (2:15)
12 Weekend At Trouville (Orchestra) (2:30)
13 I Remember It Well (2:24)
14 About Gigi (4:48)
15 Gaston's Soliloquy (2:53)
16 Gigi (3:53)
17 I'm Glad I'm Not Young Any More (3:15)
18 Say A Prayer For Me Tonight (2:58)

Total album length: 49 minutes

Original Soundtrack

Lyrics by   Music by
M-G-M presents Alan Jay Lerner - Frederick Loewe

An Arthur Freed Production

66 Love Me Or Leave Me

| • **Album sales:** Under 500,000 | • **Highest position:** 1 (17 weeks) | • **Release date:** June 1955 |

The actor and singer Doris Day was at the height of her fame when she recorded *Love Me Or Leave Me*, the soundtrack to her film of the same name. The movie was a musical based on the life of Ruth Etting, a successful pop singer of the 1920s and 1930s, who had recorded lively jazz-influenced hit versions of songs like McCarthy and Monaco's 'You Made Me Love You' and, of course, Kahn and Donaldson's track 'Love Me Or Leave Me'.

Doris Day neither looked or sounded much like Ruth Etting but – as with Diana Ross's later portrayal of Billie Holiday in *Lady Sings The Blues* – this was in many ways an advantage, as the public weren't forced to make a direct comparison between the singers.

As it was, the songs were ideally suited to Doris Day's style (it's easy to forget that she was a jazz singer before becoming an actress). Some critics found arranger Percy Faith's recreation of the 1920's music styles overbearing at times, but none could deny the sheer exuberance of Doris Day's performance. Neither could the public. *Love Me Or Leave Me* went straight to Number One in the summer of 1955 and stayed there for a remarkable 17 weeks.

Number One singles:	**Personnel:**
None	Doris Day
	James Cagney (d. 1986)
Grammy awards:	Percy Faith (d. 1976)
None	Audrey Young
	Peter Leeds
Label: US: Columbia	Harry Bellaver
Recorded in: N/A	**Producer:** N/A

1   Overture (1:34)
2   It All Depends On You (2:02)
3   You Made Me Love You (I Didn't Want to Do It) (2:29)
4   Stay On The Right Side, Sister (1:00)
5   Everybody Loves My Baby (1:11)
6   Mean To Me (2:12)
7   Sam, The Old Accordion Man (2:06)
8   Shaking The Blues Away (3:30)
9   (What Can I Say) After I Say I'm Sorry?/I Cried for You/My Blue Heaven (4:13)
10 I'll Never Stop Loving You (1:55)
11 Never Look Back (2:26)
12 At Sundown (1:31)
13 Love Me Or Leave Me (2:14)
14 Finale (0:19)

Total album length: 29 minutes

ACS 8773

ELECTRONICALLY RE-CHANNELED FOR **STEREO**

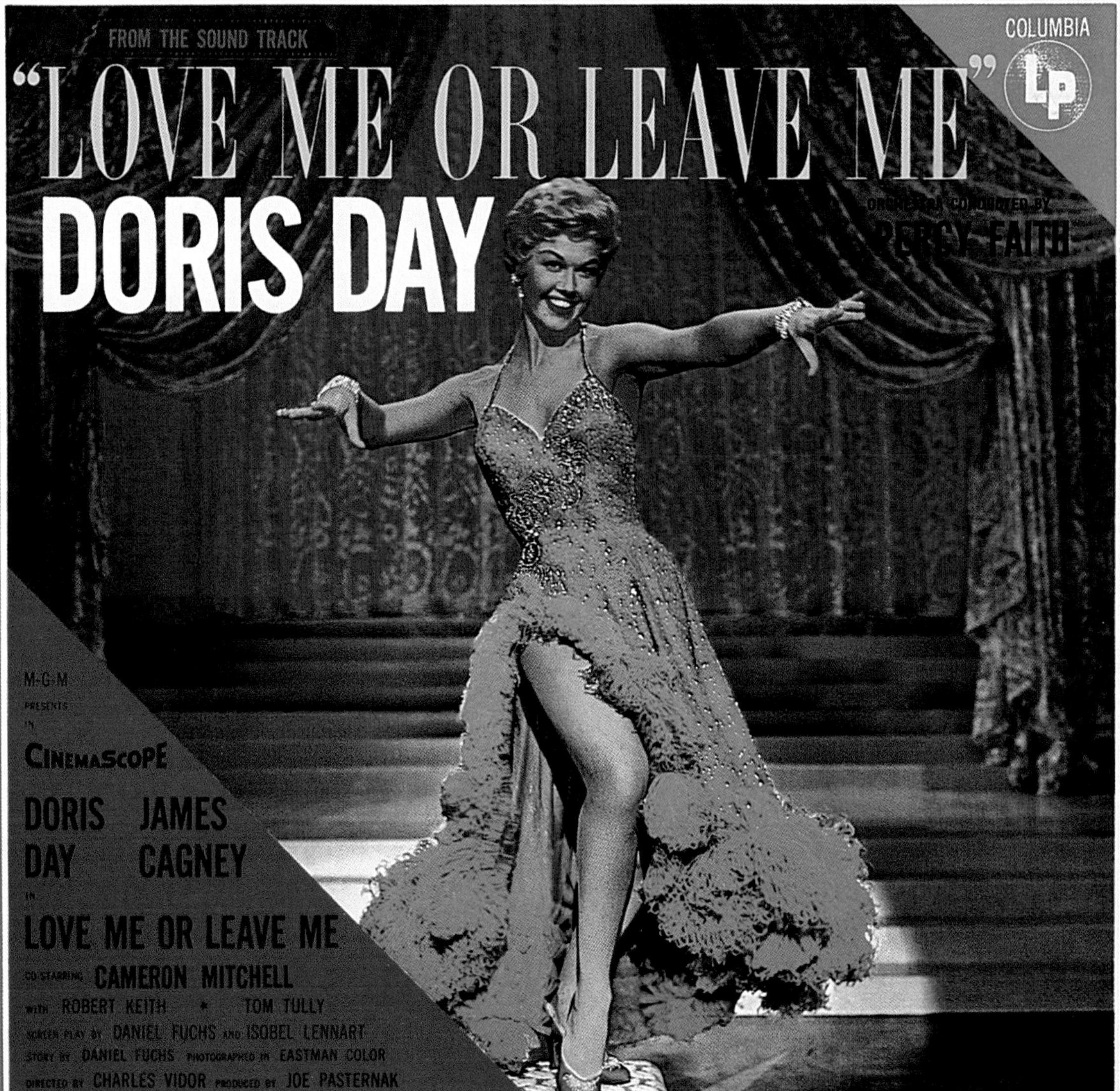

Favorites In Hi-Fi

| • **Album sales:** 500,000 | • **Highest position:** 40 | • **Release date:** 1958 |

Jeanette Macdonald and Nelson Eddy achieved lasting fame with their appearances in series of MGM films during the late 1930s and early 1940s. The last of these film collaborations, 'I Married An Angel', was released in 1942. When the pair were re-united for a TV special in 1956, they had not sung together for 14 years. The public reaction to their performance was so overwhelming that RCA promptly signed them up to record a reunion album – *Favorites In Hi-Fi*.

Both MacDonald and Eddy were accomplished singers. Eddy had started as an opera singer before gong into the movies while MacDonald had gone from Broadway to Hollywood to opera. For the *Favorites In Hi-Fi* album, they decided against springing any surprises. Instead, they gave a nostalgic audience precisely what they wanted – light operatic favorites like 'Giannina Mia' and 'Ah, Sweet Mystery Of Life'. Sadly this was to be the only recording to come out of their brief reunion. Soon afterwards Jeannette MacDonald became too ill from heart trouble to sing, eventually dying in 1965, two years before her singing partner.

Despite spending only one week on the charts, *Favorites in Hi-Fi* was a consistent seller that eventually earned the duo a gold disc.

Number One singles:
None

Grammy awards:
None

Label: US: RCA

Recorded in: New York & Hollywood, USA

Personnel:
Nelson Eddy (d. 1967)
Jeanette MacDonald
 (d. 1965)
Lehman Engel
Dave Rose

Producers:
Simon Rady
Ed Welker

1 Will You Remember
2 Rosalie
3 Giannina Mia
4 Rose-Marie
5 Italian Street Song
6 Indian Love Call
7 Ah, Sweet Mystery Of Life
8 The Breeze And I
9 While My Lady Sleeps
10 Wanting You
11 Stouthearted Men
12 Beyond The Blue Horizon

Official times not available

RCA VICTOR
LPM-1738
New Orthophonic High Fidelity Recording

JEANETTE MacDONALD & NELSON EDDY FAVORITES IN HI-FI

Will You Remember (Sweetheart) (Duet)

Rosalie (Nelson Eddy)

Giannina Mia (Jeanette MacDonald)

Rose-Marie (Nelson Eddy)

Italian Street Song (Jeanette MacDonald)

Indian Love Call (Duet)

Ah, Sweet Mystery of Life (Duet)

The Breeze and I (Jeanette MacDonald)

While My Lady Sleeps (Nelson Eddy)

Wanting You (Duet)

Stouthearted Men (Nelson Eddy)

Beyond the Blue Horizon (Jeanette MacDonald)

Photo—Herb Ball

RCA Printed in U.S.A. RE

64 Christmas With Conniff

| • Album sales: 500,000 | • Highest position: 14 | • Release date: 1959 |

Given the enthusiasm of 1950s America for the Christmas album, the release of *Christmas With Ray Conniff* was probably inevitable, sooner or later. The album is one of the most unashamedly commercial of Conniff's recordings. His initial chart hit albums like *'S Wonderful!* and *'S Marvelous* – and particularly *Concert In Rhythm* – had featured complex and sophisticated arrangements with wordless vocalising replacing the conventional lead vocal. For the Christmas album, however, Conniff treads rather closer to the singalong territory dominated by his original employer at Columbia Records, Mitch Miller.

As a result, this is an upbeat selection of secular Christmas songs, such as 'Winter Wonderland', 'Jingle Bells' and the lesser-known 'Christmas Bride', delivered with easy assurance by the Ray Conniff Singers who, this time, get to sing all the words and keep their wordless vocalising for the brief instrumental breaks.

Christmas With Conniff did indeed prove a lasting hit with the American public, but, oddly enough, not an immediate one. It only reached Number 14 on its original release in 1959, but then continued to chart every year for the next 10 years, before achieving its highest position ever (Number Seven) in 1969, by which time it had easily earned a gold record.

Number One singles: None

Grammy awards: None

Label: US: Columbia; UK: Philips

Recorded in: N/A

Personnel: Ray Conniff (d. 2002) Ray Conniff Singers

Producer: N/A

1   Here Comes Santa Claus (2:25)
2   Winter Wonderland (2:39)
3   Rudolph, The Red-Nosed Reindeer (2:13)
4   Christmas Bride (2:53)
5   Sleigh Ride (2:31)
6   Greensleeves (2:29)
7   Jingle Bells (2:46)
8   Silver Bells (2:30)
9   Frosty, The Snowman (2:21)
10 White Christmas (2:49)
11 Santa Claus Is Comin' To Town (2:29)
12 The Christmas Song (2:48)

Total album length: 33 minutes

PHILIPS

Christmas with Conniff

THE RAY CONNIFF SINGERS

THE CHRISTMAS SONG · JINGLE BELLS · WINTER WONDERLAND · SANTA CLAUS IS COMIN' TO TOWN · WHITE CHRISTMAS · SLEIGH RIDE · FROSTY THE SNOWMAN · SILVER BELLS · RUDOLPH, THE RED-NOSED REINDEER · HERE COMES SANTA CLAUS · GREENSLEEVES · CHRISTMAS BRIDE

PHILIPS

63 Music For The Love Hours

| • Album sales: 500,000 | • Highest position: 13 | • Release date: 1956 |

*M*usic For The Love Hours was the most individually successful of the actor and comedian Jackie Gleason's string of hit albums recorded between 1953 and 1957. It followed the now established formula set up by the first in the series, *Music For Lovers Only*, though this time the title hints more explicitly than ever as to just why the public snapped up Gleason's albums. This was music single-mindedly designed to provide a soundtrack to seduction.

Gleason himself neatly summed up his rationale for making the records: 'Every time I ever watched Clark Gable do a love scene in the movies, I'd hear this really pretty music, real romantic, come up behind him and help set the mood. So I'm figuring that if Clark Gable needs that kinda help, then a guy in Canarsie has gotta be dyin' for somethin' like this!' To this end he assembled an orchestra under the direction of Pete King and set them to work recording a set of romantic standards, including the likes of 'Serenade In Blue' and 'Just A Memory'.

Music For The Love Hours saw Gleason getting the formula right to the extent that it earned him his only gold record.

Number One singles:
None

Grammy awards:
None

Label: US: Capitol

Recorded in: N/A

Personnel:
Pete King
Bobby Hackett

Producer:
Jackie Gleason (d. 1987)

1 Darn That Dream
2 Poor Butterfly
3 Serenade In Blue
4 How Did She Look?
5 Moonlight Becomes
6 Just One More Chance
7 I Love You Much TooMuch
8 Hold Me
9 Get Out Of Town
10 Our Love
11 Just A Memory
12 If I Could Be With You
13 Ghost Of A Chance
14 I've Got You Under My Skin
15 Lover Come Back To Me
16 The House Is Haunted

Official times not available

Jackie Gleason

JACKIE GLEASON presents
music for
the Love Hours
Capitol
RECORDS
CAPITOL RECORDS
HIGH FIDELITY
RECORDING

62 Folk Songs Sing Along With Mitch

| • **Album sales:** 500,000 | • **Highest position:** 11 | • **Release date:** 1959 |

By the time *Folk Songs Sing Along With Mitch* was released in the summer of 1959, the Sing Along Series, masterminded by Columbia's head of A&R Mitch Miller, was well on the way to becoming a national institution.

Even a winning formula has to be varied from time to time and, with his dual role as artist and record company executive, Mitch Miller was well attuned to the changing fashions in music. Folk music was coming into vogue and so, for this fifth album in the series, Mitch Miller And The Gang decided to root around for some traditional classics. The songs they came up with, having canvassed scout groups across the nation, are very much oriented towards the kind of folk songs most commonly sung to small children – from 'Oh Susanna' to 'Pop Goes The Weasel'. As

a result *Folk Songs Sing Along* was the most child-centred selection to date.

The change may have initially disconcerted the *Sing Along* audience a little, as the album only charted at Number 11. However, the public clearly soon got used to it as it remained in the charts for 31 weeks and went on to go gold, like all its predecessors.

Number One singles: None	**Recorded in:** New York, USA
Grammy awards: None	**Personnel:** Mitch Miller And The Gang
Label: US: Columbia; UK: Philips	**Producer:** Mitch Miller

1 **My Darling Clementine**
2 **On Top Of Old Smoky**
3 **Goodnight Irene**
4 **Down In The Valley**
5 **Aunt Rhody**
6 **Red River Valley**
7 **Listen To The Mocking Bird**
8 **When Johnny Comes Marching Home**
9 **Medley: Pop Goes The Weasel / Skip To My Lou**
10 **Medley: Oh Susanna / Camptown Races**
11 **Medley: Billy Boy / The Bear Went Over The Mountain**
12 **The Blue Tail Fly**

Official times not available

FOLK SONGS

SING ALONG WITH MITCH

MITCH MILLER AND THE GANG

MY DARLING CLEMENTINE  ON TOP OF OLD SMOKY GOODNIGHT, IRENE DOWN IN THE VALLEY · AUNT RHODY RED RIVER VALLEY LISTEN TO THE MOCKING BIRD WHEN JOHNNY COMES MARCHING HOME POP! GOES THE WEASEL · SKIP TO MY LOU · OH, SUSANNA! CAMPTOWN RACES BILLY BOY THE BEAR WENT OVER THE MOUNTAIN THE BLUE TAIL FLY

61 More Songs Of The Fabulous Fifties

| • **Album sales:** 500,000 | • **Highest position:** 11 | • **Release date:** May 1959 |

Roger Williams

Boxer turned musician Roger Williams was born Louis Wertz and named after the pilgrim father by his label boss Dave Kapp. A classically trained pianist, he had scored a major hit with *Songs Of The Fabulous Fifties*. Now he decided to give the public more of what they evidently wanted, and returned with a follow-up album, *More Songs Of The Fabulous Fifties*.

As before, the songs he chose were a mixture of pop standards, such as 'Moonglow', 'Young At Heart', and 'Unchained Melody', together with hit songs from recent musicals, like 'Three Coins In The Fountain' and the 'Theme From Picnic'. These were supplemented by the very slightest of deviations into country music with a version of Pee Wee King's 'Tennessee Waltz'. And just to make sure the album was a hit, Williams rounded it off with his own 'song of the fabulous fifties',

'Autumn Leaves', which had yielded him a Number One single back in 1955.

More Songs Of The Fabulous Fifties didn't quite match the success of its predecessor, only reaching Number 11 during a 14-week stay on the Billboard album charts on its release in 1959. However, it did prove a consistent enough seller to eventually be awarded a gold disc.

Number One singles:
None

Grammy awards:
None

Label: US: Kapp

Recorded in: N/A

Personnel:
Roger Williams

Producer: N/A

1   **Moonglow**
2   **Theme From Picnic**
3   **Unchained Melody**
4   **Tennessee Waltz**
5   **Hey There**
6   **April In Portugal**
7   **My Heart Cries For You**
8   **True Love**
9   **La Vie En Rose**
10 **Three Coins In The Fountain**
11 **Young At Heart**
12 **I Believe**
13 **Autumn Leaves**

Official times not available

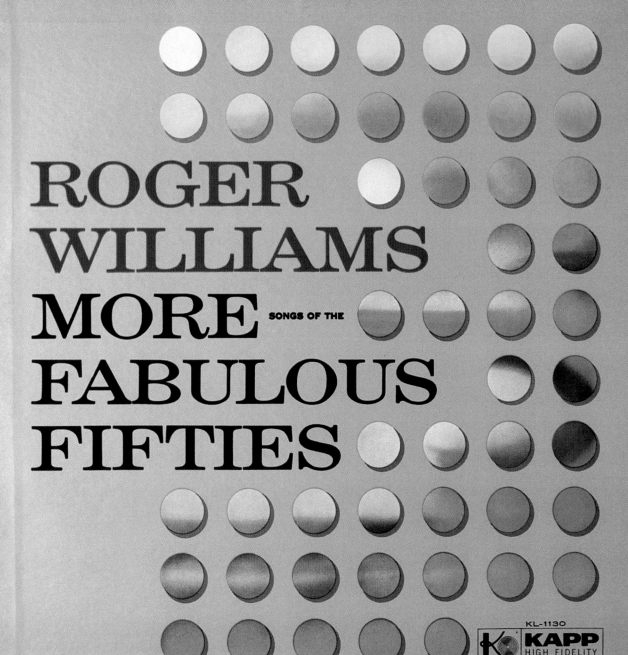

ROGER
WILLIAMS
MORE SONGS OF THE
FABULOUS
FIFTIES

©1959 Kapp, Printed in U.S.A.

KL-1130

KAPP
HIGH FIDELITY

60 'S Marvellous

| • **Album sales:** 500,000 | • **Highest position:** 10 | • **Release date:** November 1957 |

With the album *'S Marvellous*, arranger and conductor Ray Conniff settled on the sound that was to become his hallmark for more than 40 years and would allow him to sell more than 50 million records worldwide over that time.

In the mid-1950s Ray Conniff was a staff arranger for Columbia (working under the direction of the formidable Mitch Miller). His success arranging for Johnny Mathis persuaded Miller to let Conniff make his own records. The first of these, *'S Wonderful*, had seen Conniff mix a gentle rhythm section with strings and brass as the backdrop for his particular innovation – a vocal ensemble sing wordless melodies over the top. The record was a sizeable hit but, for reasons best known to himself, Conniff decided to follow it with an album of light instrumental rock'n'roll called *Dance The Bop*.

When that flopped, Ray Conniff promptly made *'S Marvellous* as a sequel to *'S Wonderful.* The album featured the same mix of show tunes and pop standards, featuring songs by composers such as Gershwin, Cole Porter and Richard Rodgers, with Glenn Miller's big band number 'Moonlight Serenade' thrown in for slight variation. The result was an album that comfortably outsold its predecessor, notching up 31 weeks on the chart and eventually going gold.

Number One singles: None	**Recorded in:** N/A
Grammy awards: None	**Personnel:** Ray Conniff (d. 2002) Ray Conniff Singers
Label: US: Columbia	**Producer:** N/A

1 **The Way You Look Tonight** (3:08)
2 **I Hear A Rhapsody** (2:19)
3 **They Can't Take That Away From Me** (3:04)
4 **Moonlight Serenade** (2:47)
5 **I Love You** (3:29)
6 **I've Told Ev'ry Little Star** (2:53)
7 **You Do Something To Me** (2:39)
8 **As Time Goes By** (2:58)
9 **In The Still Of The Night** (3:02)
10 **Someone To Watch Over Me** (2:58)
11 **Be My Love** (3:10)
12 **Where Or When** (3:19)

Total album length: 36 minutes

Ray Conniff

& His Orchestra

's Marvellous

The Way You Look Tonight
I Hear A Rhapsody
They Can't Take That Away From Me
Moonlight Serenade
I Love You
I've Told Ev'ry Little Star
You Do Something To Me
As Time Goes By
In The Still Of The Night
Someone To Watch Over Me
Be My Love
Where Or When

STEREO

59 Concert In Rhythm

| • **Album sales:** 500,000 | • **Highest position:** 9 | • **Release date:** August 1958 |

Big band veteran turned pop arranger Ray Conniff showed another side to his musical abilities with his 1958 album *Concert In Rhythm*. This time, rather than take pop songs or show tunes and give them arrangements that suggested something of the depth of classical music, he decided to reverse the process: for this album, he took classical themes and set out to give them something of the sheen and catchiness, not to mention rhythm, of pop songs.

It's an idea that became increasingly popular through the 1950s and 1960s, with the likes of 101 Strings and Jacques Loussier Trio trying their hands, but Conniff was undoubtedly in there at the beginning. The tunes Coniff picked to include are mostly of the instantly familiar kind – 'Rhapsody In Blue', 'Theme From *Swan Lake*',

'Rachmaninoff's Second' and so on. Conniff's arrangements followed his now established style: discreet drums, swelling strings and brass provide the backdrop, while the melody lines are carried by the wordless vocalising of the Ray Conniff singers, sometimes augmented by a solo piano. *Concert In Rhythm* earned Conniff a gold disc.

1 **Favorite Theme From Tchaikovsky's First Piano Concerto (2:57)**
2 **Favorite Theme From Tchaikovsky's *Swan Lake* Ballet (2:46)**
3 **Favorite Theme From Rachmaninoff's Second Piano Concerto (2:22)**
4 **Favorite Theme From Tchaikovsky's Fifth Symphony (2:46)**
5 **Early Evening (Theme From The Ray Conniff Suite) (2:33)**
6 **Favorite Theme From Tchaikovsky's *Romeo And Juliet* (2:43)**
7 **Rhapsody In Blue (2:56)**
8 **I'm Always Chasing Rainbows (From Chopin's 'Fantasy Impromptu') (2:18)**
9 **The Lamp Is Low (From Ravel's 'Pavane For A Dead Princess') (3:14)**
10 **On The Trail (From Grofe's 'Grand Canyon Suite') (2:47)**
11 **My Reverie (From Debussy's 'Reverie') (2:54)**
12 **Schubert's Serenade (2:31)**

Total album length: 33 minutes

Number One singles: None	**Label:** US: Columbia; UK: Philips
Grammy Awards: None	**Personnel:** Ray Conniff (d. 2002) Ray Conniff Singers
Recorded in: N/A	**Producer:** N/A

RAY CONNIFF
and his orchestra and chorus

CONCERT IN RHYTHM

PHILIPS

Sleeve artwork by Jon Abbot

Song Hits From Theatreland

| • **Album sales:** 500,000 | • **Highest position:** 8 | • **Release date:** 1955 |

The biggest-selling British musical export to the USA prior to the Beatles was, remarkably enough, Annunzio Paolo Mantovani. Mantovani, a violinist turned bandleader and conductor, was born in Venice, Italy, but brought up in London, England. Mantovani began to release records during the 1930s, but it was only in 1951, with his hit 'Charmaine', that he really implanted himself in the American consciousness. This was a haunting instrumental that showcased what was to become Mantovani's trademark, the shimmering 'cascading strings' devised by arranger Ronald Binge.

It was with the coming of the long-playing album, though, that Mantovani really came into his own. His first big hit album was this collection of favourites from the great stage musicals. It is almost entirely made up of love songs, from Rodgers and Hart's 1930s' classic 'Bewitched' (from *Pal Joey*) via Rodgers and Hammerstein's 'Some Enchanted Evening' (taken from the big hit musical of the moment *South Pacific*), right through to Irving Berlin's 'They Say It's Wonderful' (from *Annie Get Your Gun*).

Song Hits From Theatreland was a solid if unspectacular chart hit, peaking at a respectable Number Eight, but its continued sales over the years saw the album eventually win a gold disc.

Number One singles: None	**Recorded in:** N/A
Grammy awards: None	**Personnel:** Annunzio Paolo Mantovani (d. 1980)
Label: UK: Decca	**Producers:** N/A

1 **If I Loved You**
2 **Wunderbar**
3 **I've Never Been In Love Before**
4 **Bewitched**
5 **I Talk To The Trees**
6 **Some Enchanted Evening**
7 **Out Of My Dreams**
8 **Strangers In Paradise**
9 **C'est Magnifique**
10 **Almost Like Being In Love**
11 **Hello Young Lovers**
12 **They Say It's Wonderful**

Official times not available

Mantovani

MANTOVANI SONG HITS FROM THEATRELAND

DECCA
STEREO PHONIC
SKL 4037

Guys and Dolls
Paint Your Wag...
Can — Can
Pal Joey · Kismet
Brigadoon
The King and I
Oklahoma
Annie Get Your Gun
South Pacific
Kiss Me Kate
Carousel

57 Porgy And Bess

| • **Album sales:** 500,000 | • **Highest position:** 8 | • **Release date:** August 1959 |

George Gershwin's classic folk opera *Porgy And Bess* came to the screen in 1959. Although it boasted some of the leading African-American actors of the day, including Sidney Poitier as Porgy and Dorothy Dandridge as Bess, it received mixed reviews. Director Otto Preminger was accused by some critics, including Gershwin's estate, of having trivialized the work. However, the soundtrack, featuring such classics as 'Summertime' and 'It Ain't Necessarily So', proved popular. It reached Number Eight on the Billboard album chart on its release in 1959, and remained there for 47 weeks.

Gershwin wrote the music for the 1935 opera with the help of his brother, lyricist Ira, and DuBose Heyward, author of the original novel. The story centres around the poor black community of Catfish Row: Porgy, a cripple, falls in love with Bess, a beautiful but troubled drug addict. The tragic tale of Bess's rejection of Porgy and her flight to New York City with the drug dealer Sportin' Life, played in the movie by Sammy Davis Jnr, provides a backdrop for many moving songs, sung in this version by Robert McFerrin and Adele Addison, who dubbed the voices of Poitier and Dandridge respectively.

Number One singles:
None

Grammy awards:
None

Label: US: Columbia

Recorded in: N/A

Personnel:
Robert McFerrin
Adele Addison
André Previn

Producers: N/A

1   Overture
2   Summertime
3   I Wants To Stay Here
4   My Man's Gone Now
5   I Got Plenty O' Nuttin'
6   Buzzard Song
7   Bess, You Is My Woman Now
8   It Ain't Necessarily So
9   What You Want Wid Bess?
10 Woman Is A Sometime Thing
11 Oh, Doctor Jesus
12 Medley: Here Come de Honey Man/Crab Man/Oh, Dey's So Fresh And Fine
13 There's A Boat Dat'A Leavin' Soon For New York
14 Oh Bess, Oh Where's My Bess?
15 Oh, Lawd, I'm On My Way!

Official times not available

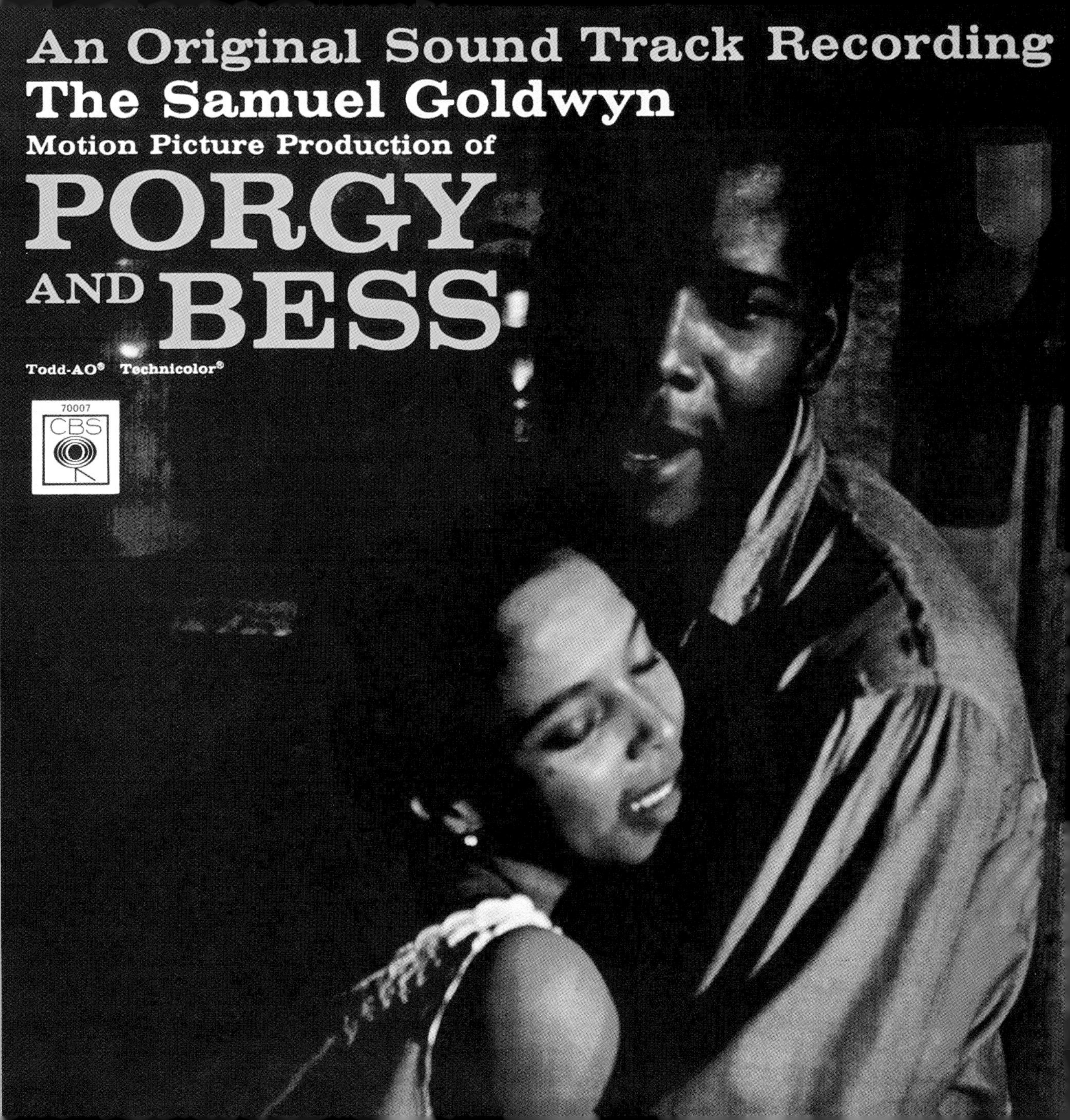

An Original Sound Track Recording
The Samuel Goldwyn
Motion Picture Production of
PORGY
AND BESS

Todd-AO® Technicolor®

70007

56 Strauss Waltzes

| • Album sales: 500,000 | • Highest position: 7 | • Release date: 1953 |

The popularity of the Italian-born Annunzio Paolo Mantovani had reached such a peak in the USA by the late 1950s that even records he had recorded some years earlier started to appear on the album charts.

One such was his collection of Strauss Waltzes. This was originally recorded for the Decca label in 1953. However, a new release of the album in stereo format was enough to propel it into the charts. This was a tribute to the care which Mantovani lavished on the recording process; rarely had an orchestra been recorded with such a bright, clear sound as Mantovani now achieved. For early owners of the new stereo hi-fis, a Mantovani album was almost a compulsory purchase, if only to demonstrate the capabilities of the equipment.

Mantovani's collection of Strauss Waltzes offers precisely what his listeners had come to expect. It begins with the 'Blue Danube' and ends with 'Du Und Du' from perhaps Strauss' best known opera, *Die Fleidermaus*. Along the way his 40-piece orchestra show off their distinctively vivid cascading strings.

Strauss Waltzes only reached Number Seven on the charts but managed to sell consistently highly enough over a long enough period of time to earn Mantovani a gold record.

Number One singles:	Recorded in: N/A
None	
	Personnel:
Grammy awards:	Annunzio Paolo Mantovani
None	(d. 1980)
Label: UK: Decca	Producers: N/A

1 **Blue Danube** (3:20)
2 **Voices Of Spring, OP 410** (2:57)
3 **Roses Of The South** (3:13)
4 **Emperor Waltz, OP 437** (3:09)
5 **A Thousand And One Nights** (6:01)
6 **Treasure Waltz (From *The Gipsy Baron*)** (1:55)
7 **Village Swallows** (3:14)
8 **Wine, Women, And Song, OP 333** (3:09)
9 **Acceleration Waltz** (3:14)
10 **Tales From The Vienna Woods** (3:24)
11 **Morgenblatter** (3:13)
12 **Du Und Du (from *Die Fledermaus*)** (3:09)

Total album length: 40 minutes

Mantovani

MANTOVANI
& his orchestra
Strauss Waltzes

DECCA

55 Blue Hawaii

| • **Album sales:** 500,000 | • **Highest position:** 7 | • **Release date:** May 1959 |

By the late 1950s Billy Vaughn had emerged as the only bandleader who was able to come to terms with the rock 'n' roll era. He specialized in taking the familiar sound of the big band and grafting on the trademarks of the rock-'n'-roll sound – stressing the roles of drums and saxophone, particularly the latter. At the heart of the arrangements that Vaughn crafted was his 'twin-sax' sound: this consisted of one alto sax playing the melody, a second alto shadowing it, playing a third above, then a battery of four tenor saxes providing the counterpoint.

A year prior to the release of *Blue Hawaii*, Billy Vaughn had had his first big hit album with *Sail Along Silv'ry Moon,* which had gone gold. Since then, however, his album sales had declined somewhat. So with *Blue Hawaii*, Vaughn decided to do something a little different and devote a whole album to Hawaiian-inspired material. The resultant mixture of show tunes and folk tunes certainly caught the public imagination and gave Vaughn one of the biggest hit albums of his lengthy career. It peaked at Number Seven in the charts but stayed there for almost a year, earning Vaughn his second gold record.

Number One singles:	Recorded in: N/A
None	
	Personnel:
Grammy awards:	Billy Vaughn (d. 1991)
None	
	Producer: N/A
Label: US: Dot	

1   **The Hawaiian Wedding Song**
2   **Cocoanut Grove**
3   **Isle Of Golden Dreams**
4   **Little Brown Gal**
5   **Hawaiian Paradise**
6   **My Little Grass Shack**
7   **Trade Winds**
8   **Blue Hawaii**
9   **Sweet Leilani**
10 **Hawaiian War Chant**
11 **Song Of The Islands**
12 **Beyond The Reef**
13 **Hawaiian Sunset**
14 **Aloha Oe**

Official times not available

DLP 25165

STEREO

BLUE HAWAII
BILLY VAUGHN

THE HAWAIIAN WEDDING SONG
COCOANUT GROVE
ISLE OF GOLDEN DREAMS
LITTLE BROWN GAL
HAWAIIAN PARADISE
MY LITTLE GRASS SHACK
TRADE WINDS
BLUE HAWAII
SWEET LEILANI
HAWAIIAN WAR CHANT
SONG OF THE ISLANDS
BEYOND THE REEF
HAWAIIAN SUNSET
ALOHA OE

Dot
RECORDS

ULTRA HIGH-FIDELITY

54 Party Sing Along With Mitch

• **Album sales:** 500,000 | • **Highest position:** 7 | • **Release date:** 1959

*P*arty Sing Along With Mitch was the sixth instalment in the *Sing Along* Series. After the faint dip in popularity suffered by the previous instalment, *Folk Songs Sing Along*, *Party Sing Along* saw producer Mitch Miller returning to the tried-and-tested formula of the earlier volumes.

There is a mixture here of parlour songs, children's songs, numbers from musical theatre and the odd traditional ballad. The only criteria for a song's inclusion was that it should be familiar to as large a section of the American public as possible – and for those who didn't know all the words a lyric sheet was included.

What Miller had realized was that for the American public in the late 1950s – at least for those who could afford long-playing records – this really was a time of home and family and white-picket-fence values. These albums provided the perfect accompaniment to the American Dream. The only innovation on this volume was a slight increase in the number of songs – up from 12 to 16. The result was an album that made Number Seven in the charts, remained there for over a year and garnered Miller his sixth successive gold record.

Number One Singles: None	**Label:** Columbia
Grammy awards: None	**Personnel:** Mitch Miller And The Gang
Recorded in: New York, USA	**Producer:** Mitch Miller

1 The Sweetest Story Ever Told
2 I'll Take You Home Again, Kathleen
3 I Love You Truly
4 Home Sweet Home
5 Ramblin' Wreck From Georgia Tech
6 I Wonder Who's Kissing Her Now
7 A Bird In A Gilded Cage
8 In The Shade Of The Old Apple Tree
9 Sweet Rosie O'Grady
10 School Days
11 Medley: My Gal Sal / In The Good Old Summer Time
12 Medley: Harrigan / Wait Till The Sun Shines Nelly
13 Goodnight Ladies
14 Medley: The Sidewalks Of New York / Meet Me Tonight In Dreamland
15 Cuddle Up A Little Closer
16 Oh! What A Pal Was Mary

Official times not available

PARTY
SING ALONG WITH MITCH

(Includes Special Sing-Along Lyric Sheets)

Photographer: Barrett Gallagher

MITCH MILLER AND THE GANG · THE SWEETEST STORY EVER TOLD
I'LL TAKE YOU HOME AGAIN, KATHLEEN · I LOVE YOU TRULY
HOME, SWEET HOME · RAMBLIN' WRECK FROM GEORGIA TECH
I WONDER WHO'S KISSING HER NOW · A BIRD IN A GILDED CAGE
· IN THE SHADE OF THE OLD APPLE TREE · SWEET ROSIE O'GRADY
SCHOOL DAYS · MY GAL SAL · IN THE GOOD OLD SUMMERTIME
HARRIGAN · WAIT TILL THE SUN SHINES NELLIE · GOODNIGHT, LADIES
THE SIDEWALKS OF NEW YORK · MEET ME TONIGHT IN DREAMLAND
CUDDLE UP A LITTLE CLOSER ♥♥♥ OH! WHAT A PAL WAS MARY

CL 1331

53 Songs Of The Fabulous Fifties

• **Album sales:** 500,000 │ • **Highest position:** 6 │ • **Release date:** February 1957 │

With albums like *Songs Of The Fabulous Fifties*, pianist Roger Williams (born Louis Wertz) presented himself as the very epitome of smooth, sophisticated easy listening – which made it all the more surprising that he should have come to music by way of boxing and a stint in the navy, before winning a TV talent contest and launching his career with the best-selling single 'Autumn Leaves'.

Recorded in 1957, when the decade was little more than halfway through, *Songs Of The Fabulous Fifties*' title suggests an upbeat, optimistic mood, and the record itself backs up that impression. There's a whole range of hit songs from the previous few years here: from movie themes like 'High Noon' to pop ballads like 'Mona Lisa'. There is even the odd folk song, such as 'Goodnight Irene'. Williams presents all of them in his flashy, classically-influenced style (the story goes that Williams was thrown out of his first music school when a tutor heard him playing 'Smoke Gets In Your Eyes').

The result was a collection that gave Williams his first Top Ten album, and his first gold record too, as it took up residence in the charts, remaining there for over a year.

Number One singles:
None

Grammy awards:
None

Label: US & UK: Kapp

Recorded in: N/A

Personnel:
Roger Williams
Marty Gold
Hal Kranner

Producer: N/A

1   Blue Tango
2   Vaya Con Dios
3   High Noon
4   Too Young
5   Because Of You
6   Song From Moulin Rouge
7   Mister Sandman
8   Wish You Were Here
9   Mona Lisa
10 Goodnight Irene
11 Secret Love
12 Love Is A Many Splendored Thing

Official times not available

Roger Williams

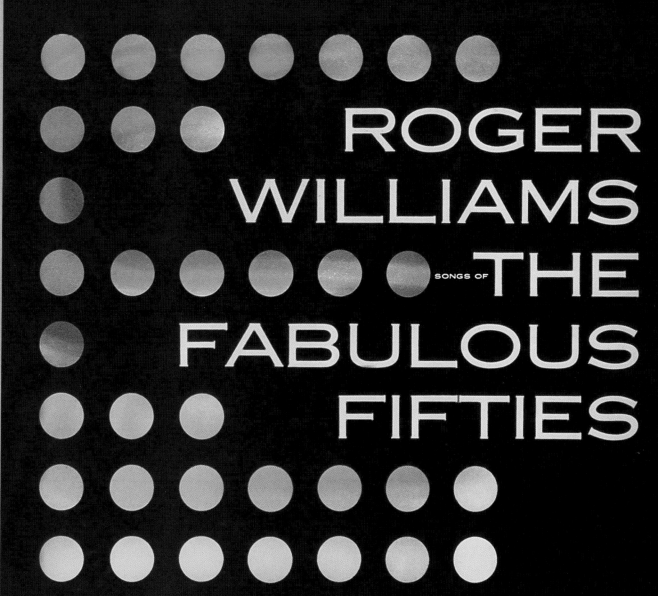

ROGER
WILLIAMS
SONGS OF THE
FABULOUS
FIFTIES

KXL-5000   KAPP
HIGH FIDELITY

52 Swing Softly

| • **Album sales:** 500,000 | • **Highest position:** 6 | • **Release date:** 1958 |

Johnny Mathis' sixth album couldn't have come at a more auspicious moment in his career. His producer Mitch Miller's imaginative policy of keeping his singles and albums separate had just paid big dividends with Mathis' *Greatest Hits* album, which remained a constant on the charts until well into the 1960s.

So how to follow up such a huge hit? Miller decided to raise the tempo and let Mathis swing a little – though, as the title suggests, not too vigorously. Mathis' regular arranger Percy Faith once again did the honours and Mathis and Miller selected a typical mixture of show tunes, such as 'Get Me To The Church On Time' and 'Its De-Lovely', together with pop classics like

'You'd Be So Nice To Come Home To' and 'I've Got The World On A String'. The result was an album explicitly designed to compete with the great commercial swinger of the time, Frank Sinatra (whom Miller had dropped from the Columbia roster back in 1952).

Swing Softly was an immediate hit. It spent a creditable 16 weeks on the US charts, peaking at Number Six, and became Johnny Mathis' third album to go gold. It remains one of his most distinctive recordings.

Number One singles:
None

Grammy awards:
None

Label: US:
Columbia/Fontana

Recorded in: New York,
USA

Personnel:
Johnny Mathis
Percy Faith and His
  Orchestra

Producer:
Mitch Miller

1 **You Hit The Spot** (2:45)
2 **It's De-Lovely** (2:53)
3 **Get Me To The Church On Time** (2:48)
4 **Like Someone In Love** (1:46)
5 **You'd Be So Nice To Come Home To** (2:41)
6 **Love Walked In** (2:13)
7 **This Heart Of Mine** (2:37)
8 **To Be In Love** (2:31)
9 **Sweet Lorraine** (3:01)
10 **Can't Get Out Of This Mood** (2:24)
11 **I've Got The World On A String** (3:08)
12 **Easy To Say (But So Hard To Do)** (2:43)

Total album length: 31 minutes

full stereo

JOHNNY MATHIS

ORCHESTRA UNDER
THE DIRECTION
OF PERCY FAITH

Swing Softly

51 Spirituals

• **Album sales:** 500,000 | • **Highest position:** 5 | • **Release date:** April 1957

*H*ymns, Tennessee Ernie Ford's first album to be exclusively devoted to religious material, had proved an unexpected and extraordinary success. One of the first long-playing records ever to sell a million copies, it had tapped a previously unsuspected market for popular devotional recordings.

There was little question as to how Tennessee Ernie Ford would follow this up. He returned almost immediately to the studio, once again accompanied by his regular arranger Jack Fascinato and dug once more into his religious repertoire. This time, however, as the title suggests, he decided to perform a set of spirituals – religious songs with roots in the folk tradition – rather than hymns. The result was

another huge success as Ford's easy baritone led the way though such popular devotional songs as 'Take My Hand, Precious Lord' and 'Peace In The Valley', accompanied by simple acoustic guitar and a vocal chorus.

Hitting the charts just a month after *Hymns* – production schedules being a lot faster in the 1950s than they are today – *Spirituals* didn't quite match the sales of its predecessor, but it made its way to Number Five in the charts. It remained there for 39 weeks.

Number One singles:
None

Grammy awards:
None

Label: US: Capitol

Recorded in: Los Angeles, USA

Personnel:
Tennessee Ernie Ford
(d. 1991)
Jack Fascinato

Producer: N/A

1   **Just A Closer Walk With Thee** (2:20)
2   **I Want To Be Ready** (2:31)
3   **Take My Hand, Precious Lord** (3:16)
4   **Stand By Me** (3:13)
5   **When God Dips His Pen Of Love In My Heart** (2:15)
6   **Get On Board Little Children** (2:47)
7   **Noah Found Grace In The Eyes Of The Lord** (2:20)
8   **Were You There** (3:40)
9   **Peace In The Valley** (3:15)
10 **I Know The Lord Laid His Hands On Me** (1:45)
11 **Wayfaring Pilgrim** (2:36)
12 **He'll Understand And Say Well Done** (2:38)

Total album length: 33 minutes

TENNESSEE ERNIE FORD
SPIRITUALS

Capitol
RECORDS

HIGH FIDELITY
RECORDING

50 Christmas Hymns And Carols

| • **Album sales:** 500,000 | • **Highest position:** 5 | • **Release date:** December 1957 |

Christmas albums made up a big part of the albums market in the 1950s; everyone from Elvis Presley to Ray Conniff recorded one. The vast majority of these records mined the same repertoire of half a dozen of the most immediately familiar Christmas carols mixed in with half-a-dozen more secular numbers.

The Robert Shaw Chorale Christmas albums, of which there were to be several over the years, offered a rather more upmarket alternative. This 1957 album, organized as eight medleys of three songs each, starts with the most recognizable songs – 'O Little Town Of Bethlehem', 'Away In A Manger', and so on – but soon moves on to more esoteric material, drawing from the folk tradition of Appalachia, France and Britain to find such pleasingly unfamiliar selections as the 'Shepherd's Carol', 'Bring A Torch, Jeanette

Isabelle' and 'I Sing Of A Maiden'.

All of them feature unusually high-class choral arrangements by Robert Shaw and his frequent collaborator Alice Parker. Public enthusiasm for the sound was such that the album peaked at Number Five in the charts on its initial release, then returned to the charts year after year till 1967, earning a gold record along the way.

Number One singles: None	**Recorded in:** N/A
Grammy awards: None	**Personnel:** Robert Shaw (d. 1999) Alice Parker
Label: US: RCA Victor	**Producer:** N/A

1   O Come All Ye Faithful/The First Nowell/O Little Town Of Bethlehem
2   O Come O Come Emanuel/ Away In A Manger/Silent Night
3   Joy To The World/It Came Upon A Midnight Clear/Angels We Have Heard On High
4   Christmas Hymn (aka Echo Hymn)/Lo How A Rose E'er Blooming/Hark The Herald Angels Sing
5   God Rest You Merry Gentlemen/My Dancing Day/I Wonder As I Wander
6   Bring A Torch Jeanette Isabelle/Patapan/We Three Kings
7   Coventry Carol/ I Sing Of A Maiden/Shepherd's Carol
8   Go Tell It On The Mountain/Carol Of The Bells/Wassail Song/Deck The Halls

Offical times not available

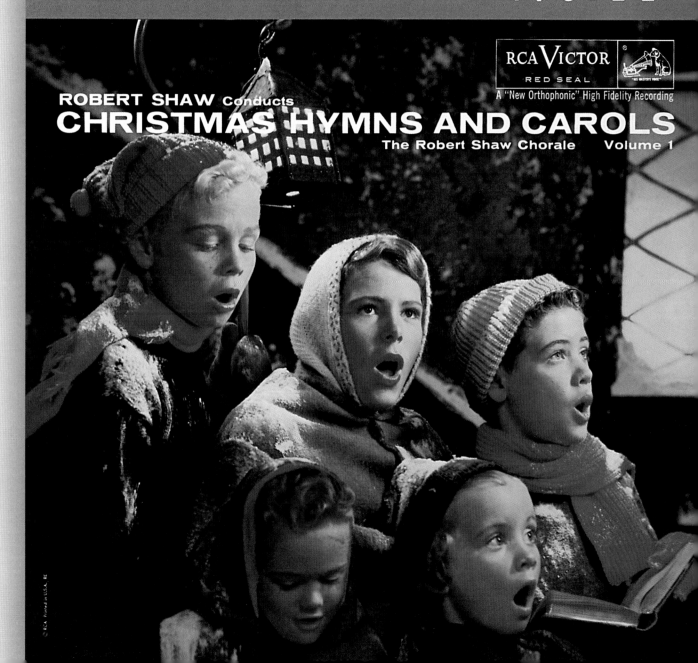

49 Sail Along Silv'ry Moon

| • Album sales: 500,000 | • Highest position: 5 | • Release date: 1958 |

At the time Kentucky-born bandleader Billy Vaughn recorded his *Sail Along Silv'ry Moon* album he was an enormously influential figure on the pop scene, as the musical director of Dot Records, the label that specialized in making sanitized cover versions of rhythm and blues hits, featuring such artists as Pat Boone, Gale Storm and the Fontane Sisters.

As a bandleader in his own right, Billy Vaughn employed the same instinct for crossing over musical styles. He took the big band sound and grafted onto it just a part of the dynamics of rock'n'roll, stressing the drums and above all the saxophones. It was the recipe for a driving catchy sound which gave Vaughn success as a singles artist too. Indeed the popularity of the *Silv'ry Moon* album was inspired by the singles

charts' success of both the dynamic 'Raunchy' and the title track. The rest of the album is rounded out with a mixture of the gentle, such as on 'Sunrise Serenade', and the danceable, such as 'Sweet Georgia Brown'.

Sail On Silv'ry Moon reached Number Five in the charts and stayed around long enough to earn a gold record, so beginning a run of 18 chart albums, stretching well into the 1960s.

Number One singles: None	**Recorded in:** California, USA
Grammy awards: None	**Personnel:** Billy Vaughn (d. 1991)
Label: US: Dot Records	**Producer:** Randy Wood

1 **Sail Along Silv'ry Moon** (2:11)
2 **Sunrise Serenade** (1:57)
3 **Sweet Georgia Brown** (2:05)
4 **Sentimental Journey** (2:27)
5 **Until Tomorrow** (2:05)
6 **Jealous** (1:56)
7 **Raunchy** (2:18)
8 **Twilight Time** (2:23)
9 **Sleepy Time Gal** (2:23)
10 **I'm Getting Sentimental Over You** (1:48)
11 **Moon Over Miami** (2:07)
12 **Tumbling Tumbleweeds** (2:03)

Total album length: 26 minutes

Billy Vaughn

DLP 3100 *Dot* ULTRA HIGH FIDELITY

BILLY VAUGHN

SAIL ALONG SILV'RY MOON

SAIL ALONG SILV'RY MOON
SUNRISE SERENADE
SWEET GEORGIA BROWN
SENTIMENTAL JOURNEY
UNTIL TOMORROW
JEALOUS
RAUNCHY
TWILIGHT TIME
SLEEPY TIME GAL
I'M GETTING SENTIMENTAL OVER YOU
MOON OVER MIAMI
TUMBLING TUMBLEWEEDS

48 West Side Story

| • **Album sales:** 500,000 | • **Highest position:** 5 | • **Release date:** March 1958 |

West Side Story is a milestone in American musical theatre, widely acclaimed as one of the greatest musicals of all time. Leonard Bernstein's musical skills, together with Stephen Sondheim's acknowledged originality as a lyricist, created the landmark production in 1957. The show ran for over 700 performances at the Winter Garden Theatre before going on tour.

The story is a musical version of Shakespeare's play *Romeo And Juliet*. Set in New York's West side, an American-born Polish boy and an immigrant Puerto Rican girl start to fall in love, but become involved in the violent warring of the street gangs around them. There was a realism and toughness about songs such as 'America' that was new to American musical theatre, but the show also contained more than its fair share of memorable romantic numbers like 'Maria', 'Tonight', and 'I Feel Pretty'.

Singers Carol Lawrence and Larry Kert were both highly praised for their lead roles in the historic production. In 1958 the Original Cast album was released and hit Number Five on the Billboard album charts.

Number One singles:
None

Grammy awards:
None

Label: US: Columbia

Recorded in: New York, USA

Producer:
Goddard Lieberson

Personnel:
Leonard Bernstein
(d. 1990)
Larry Kert (d. 1991)
Carol Lawrence
Chita Rivera
Art Smith
Marilyn Cooper
Eddie Roll
Ronnie Lee
Grover Dale
Mickey Calin
Various other personnel

1   Prologue (3:50)
2   Jet Song (2:10)
3   Something's Coming (2:40)
4   The Dance at the Gym (3:06)
5   Maria (2:40)
6   Tonight (3:53)
7   America (4:35)
8   Cool (4:01)
9   One Hand, One Heart (3:03)
10 Tonight (3:40)
11 The Rumble (2:45)
12 I Feel Pretty (2:50)
13 Somewhere (Ballet) (7:35)
14 Gee, Officer Krupke! (4:05)
15 A Boy Like That/I Have A Love (4:18)
16 Finale (2:02)

Total album length: 57 minutes

Original Cast Recording

47 Nearer The Cross

| • **Album sales:** 500,000 | • **Highest position:** 5 | • **Release date:** March 1958 |

By the summer of 1958 it was clear that Tennessee Ernie Ford's career had changed direction. The enormous success of his two devotional albums, *Hymns* and *Spirituals*, and his status as host of America's number-one rated TV show meant that his original career as a country and western singer was reaching its end. Following the summer 1957 release of *Spirituals*, Ford had gone back to secular material. It wasn't a complete flop – he did manage his last Top 20 singles hit with 'That's All' – but the two secular albums he released both failed to chart.

It was clear that the public now thought of him as a primarily religious artist. So, for his next album, Ford returned to Capitol's Hollywood studio armed with another selection of spiritual material. With a couple of exceptions – 'What A Friend We Have In Jesus', 'Nearer My God To Thee' – this was generally less familiar fare than on the previous albums, but the record-buying public didn't seem to mind.

Helped by the songs' regular airings on the TV show, *Nearer The Cross* brought Ford firmly back to the album charts, reaching Number Five during a 49-week stay and ultimately going gold.

Number One singles:
None

Grammy awards:
None

Label: US: Capitol

Recorded in: Los Angeles
USA

Personnel:
Tennessee Ernie Ford
(d. 1991)
Jack Fascinato

Producer : N/A

1   What A Friend We Have In Jesus
2   Jesus, Savior, Pilot Me
3   His Eye Is On The Sparrow
4   Beautiful Isle Of Somewhere
5   Now The Day Is Over
6   Nearer My God To Thee
7   Sweet Peace, The Gift Of God's Love
8   Whispering Hope
9   Lord, I'm Coming Home
10 I Need Thee Every Hour
11 Take Time To Be Holy
12 God Be With You

Official times not available

46 Gems Forever

| • **Album sales:** 500,000 | • **Highest position:** 5 | • **Release date:** September 1958 |

Mantovani was indisputably America's favourite light-orchestral conductor during the 1950s. His albums became synonymous with easy-listening sophistication. More than any of his contemporaries, Mantovani took a real interest in the recording process, particularly the specialized question of how best to record an orchestra, and was constantly looking to make the new microphone technology work for him.

It is this emphasis on the quality of the recorded sound that sets Mantovani's *Gems Forever* apart from most of its contemporaries. The song selection, by contrast, sees Mantovani playing very safe indeed, perhaps because his previous album, a collection of tangos, had not done as well as expected. His arrangements of show tunes were consistently his most popular

works and there is a whole array of familiar favourites here, from Lerner And Loewe's 'I Could Have Danced All Night' (from *My Fair Lady*) to George and Ira Gershwin's 'Summertime' (from *Porgy And Bess*) and Hoagy Carmichael's 'The Nearness Of You'. All of them feature Mantovani's 40-piece orchestra with its signature shimmering strings.

Gems Forever debuted on the Billboard chart in September 1958. It eventually peaked at Number Five, during a stay of over a year, and earned a gold record along the way.

Number One singles:
None

Grammy awards:
None

Label: US: London

Recorded in: N/A

Personnel:
Mantovani (d. 1980)

Producers: N/A

1   All The Things You Are (3:20)
2   True Love (3:10)
3   I Could Have Danced All Night (3:00)
4   You Keep Coming Back Like A Song (2:30)
5   A Woman In Love (2:30)
6   This Nearly Was Mine (2:40)
7   Summertime (2:45)
8   Something To Remember You By (3:20)
9   Love Letters (3:20)
10 The Nearness Of You (3:50)
11 An Affair To Remember (3:20)
12 Hey There! (3:30)

Total album length: 37 minutes

Mantovani

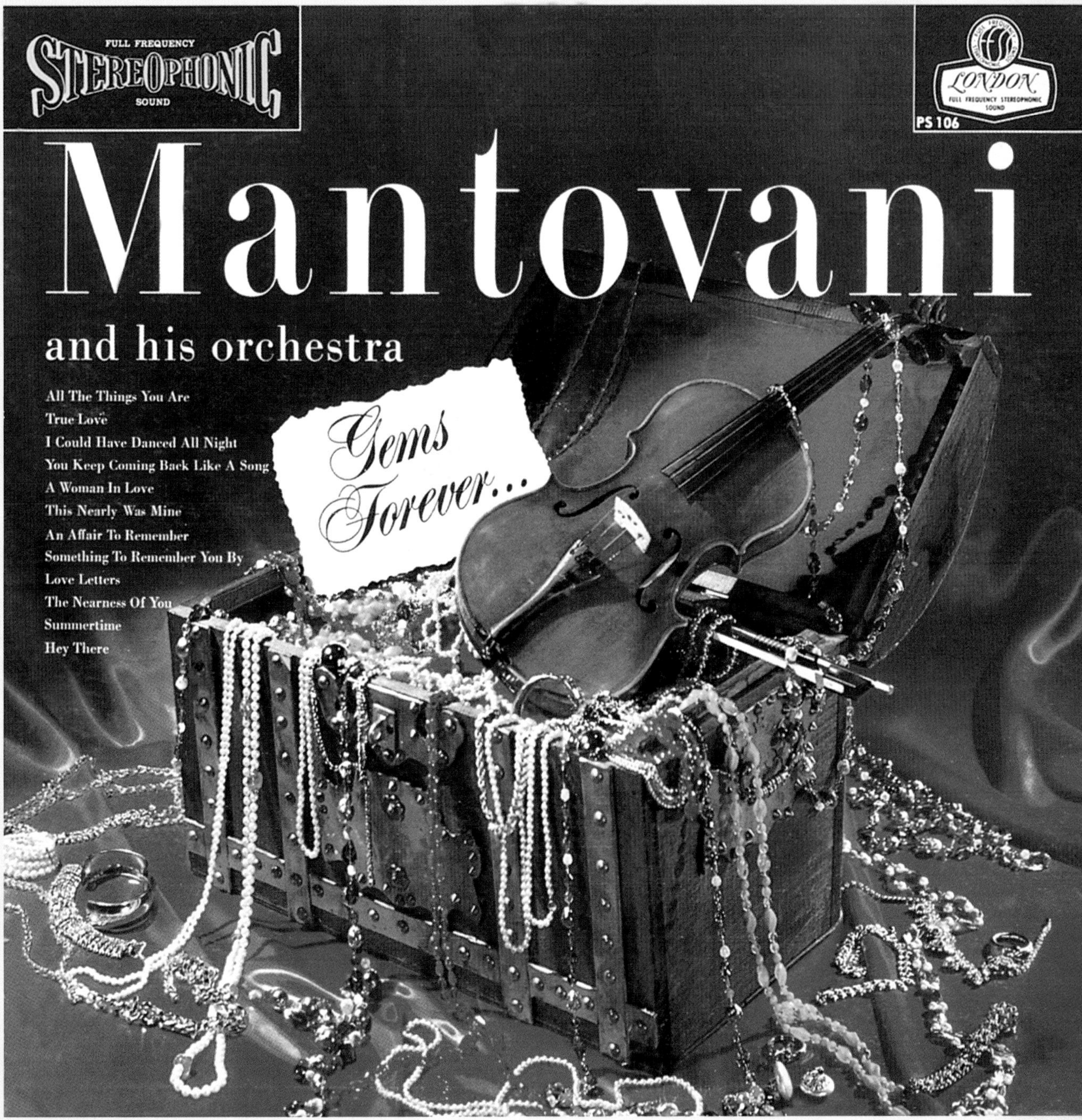

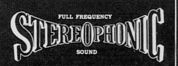

FULL FREQUENCY
STEREOPHONIC
SOUND
LONDON
FULL FREQUENCY STEREOPHONIC SOUND
PS 106
Mantovani
and his orchestra
All The Things You Are
True Love
I Could Have Danced All Night
You Keep Coming Back Like A Song
A Woman In Love
This Nearly Was Mine
An Affair To Remember
Something To Remember You By
Love Letters
The Nearness Of You
Summertime
Hey There
Gems Forever...

45 Christmas Carols

| • Album sales: 500,000 | • Highest position: 4 | • Release date: 1953 |

It was hardly surprising that Mantovani, the most popular light classical conductor of his day, would produce a Christmas album. Christmas albums were very big business indeed during the 1950s, at least in part because long-playing records were still seen as expensive luxury items – and thus ideal Christmas gifts.

Mantovani's contribution to the genre was originally recorded and released in 1953, before Billboard had started producing an albums chart. It was not until Christmas 1957 that it eventually appeared on the charts. It reappeared the following year in a brand-new stereo version and was even more successful, and continued to reappear on the charts each Christmas for several more years. Despite the title, the album is not simply devoted to Christmas carols. In

addition to the likes of 'Hark, The Herald Angels Sing' and 'The First Noel', there is also the distinctly secular 'White Christmas', and a couple of Mantovani's trademark waltzes.

The public responded with enthusiasm to Mantovani's album, and *Christmas Carols* reached Number Four in 1957. The following year it reached Number Three, and by the time of its final appearance on the charts in 1962 it had sold well enough to earn a gold record.

Number One singles:
None

Grammy awards:
None

Label: US: London

Recorded in: N/A

Personnel:
Mantovani (d. 1980)

Producers: N/A

1   The First Noel
2   Hark, The Herald Angels Sing
3   God Rest Ye Merry Gentlemen
4   White Christmas
5   Good King Wenceslas
6   O Holy Night
7   Adeste Fideles
8   Joy To The World
9   Silent Night, Holy Night
10 O Tannenbaum
11 Midnight Waltz
12 Nazareth
13 O Little Town of Bethlehem
14 Skaters Waltz

Offical times not available

MANTOVANI

Christmas Carols

The First Noel
Hark, The Herald Angels Sing
God Rest Ye Merry Gentlemen
White Christmas
Good King Wenceslas
O Holy Night
Adeste Fideles
Joy to the World
Silent Night, Holy Night
O Tannenbaum
Midnight Waltz
Nazareth
O Little Town of Bethlehem
Skaters Waltz

 ffrr **LONDON** **ffrr**

LL 913

Long playing microgroove full frequency range recording

LL 913

44 Till

• Album sales: 500,000 | **• Highest position:** 4 | **• Release date:** February 1958

Roger Williams' *Till* helped to define a particular style of easy-listening music, one which was dominated by lyrical, showy piano playing backed by light orchestral arrangements and offering a mix of show and pop tunes, with the occasional catchy classical theme.

Roger Williams (born Louis Wertz but re-christened by record-label boss David Kapp) was a childhood prodigy who studied at the Julliard School of Music before making his name on the music scene with his 1955 single 'Autumn Leaves', which spent a month at the top of the charts. The album *Till* saw Williams showing off his undoubted technical skill on the likes of 'April Love' and 'Jalousie', while offering a more restrained take on the moody 'Fascination' and 'Tammy'. Also towards the more low-key – even modernist – end of his repertoire were the two classically derived pieces here – 'Brahms' A Flat Waltz' and 'Moonlight Love' (which is based on Debussy's 'Clair de Lune').

Till was the biggest album hit of a career that has lasted until the present day and seen Williams perform for no less than eight American presidents. On its release in early in 1958, the album reached Number Four on the album charts and eventually went gold.

Number One singles:	Recorded in: N/A
None	
	Personnel:
Grammy awards:	Roger Williams
None	Marty Gold
Label: US: Kapp	Producer: N/A

1 Till
2 April Love
3 Arrivederci, Roma
4 Que Sera Sera
5 Jalousie
6 The High And Mighty
7 Fascination
8 Tammy
9 The Sentimental Touch
10 Oh, My Papa
11 Brahms' A Flat Waltz
12 Moonlight Love

Total album length: 36 minutes

Roger Williams

K-1081-S

KAPP
HIGH FIDELITY

 STEREOPHONIC SOUND

A KAPP RECORDING

TILL

APRIL LOVE

TAMMY

FASCINATION

THE HIGH AND THE MIGHTY

QUE SERA, SERA

JALOUSIE

MOONLIGHT LOVE

BRAHMS' WALTZ IN A FLAT

ARRIVIDERCI ROMA

OH, MY PAPA

SENTIMENTAL TOUCH

TILL/ROGER WILLIAMS

43 More Sing Along With Mitch

| • **Album sales:** 500,000 | • **Highest position:** 4 | • **Release date:** 1958 |

Following the runaway success of the first *Sing Along With Mitch* album, it was obvious that record company executive Miller would not take long to figure out what to do next. And that was to give the public more of what they wanted. Thus *Sing Along With Mitch* gave birth to *More Sing Along With Mitch*: Miller returned to the studio with his vocal ensemble and recorded another selection of songs direct from the American heartlands, this time including such gems as 'If You Were The Only Girl' and the 'Whiffenpoof Song'. This time he also added an Irish medley as a hint of the folk music direction that would become more pronounced in later volumes of the series.

More Sing Along With Mitch helped establish the series as the karaoke of its time. It was never intended to be any kind of musical statement, but was a case of seeing a market and filling it. Like its predecessor, the album went gold, though this time it didn't make the Number One slot, instead peaking at Number Four. More importantly however, it is, along with the rest of the series, firmly imprinted in the childhood memories of millions of Americans.

Number One singles:
None

Grammy awards:
None

Label: US: Columbia

Recorded in: New York, USA

Personnel:
Mitch Miller And The Gang

Producer:
Mitch Miller

1 **Medley: Pretty Baby/Be My Little Baby Bumble Bee** (3:48)
2 **Medley: Sweet Adeline/Let Me Call You Sweetheart** (3:34)
3 **Moonlight And Roses** (2:42)
4 **If You Were The Only Girl** (3:31)
5 **My Buddy** (3:02)
6 **The Whiffenpoof Song** (3:11)
7 **Carolina In The Morning** (2:54)
8 **Irish Medley: When Irish Eyes Are Smiling/My Wild Irish Rose** (3:37)
9 **Medley: Shine On Harvest Moon/For Me And My Gal** (2:40)
10 **You Tell Me Your Dream, I'll Tell You Mine** (2:39)
11 **There's A Long, Long Trail** (2:09)
12 **In The Evening By The Moonlight** (2:35)

Total abum length: 36 minutes

CL 1243

MORE SING ALONG WITH MITCH

MITCH MILLER AND THE GANG

Photographer: Barrett Gallagher

Sleeve artwork by Barrett Gallagher

PRETTY BABY · BE MY LITTLE BABY BUMBLE BEE · SWEET ADELINE
LET ME CALL YOU SWEETHEART · MOONLIGHT AND ROSES · IF YOU WERE THE ONLY GIRL
MY BUDDY · THE WHIFFENPOOF SONG · CAROLINA IN THE MORNING
WHEN IRISH EYES ARE SMILING · MY WILD IRISH ROSE
SHINE ON HARVEST MOON · FOR ME AND MY GAL · YOU TELL ME YOUR DREAM,
I'LL TELL YOU MINE · THERE'S A LONG, LONG TRAIL · IN THE EVENING BY THE MOONLIGHT

42 Still More Sing Along With Mitch

| • **Album sales:** 500,000 | • **Highest position:** 4 | • **Release date:** 1959 |

Still More Sing Along With Mitch was the fourth in the enormously and enduringly popular *Sing Along* Series. It followed the Number One hit *Christmas Sing Along* album, and, as its gently self-mocking title suggested, the series was now definitely here to stay.

Whether, when Mitch Miller started out as a jazz and light classical oboist in the late 1930s, he suspected that his biggest successes would come with lusty choral renditions of 'A Bicycle Made For Two' or 'Oh! You Beautiful Doll' is not known, although it seems somewhat unlikely. However Miller had not made his way up to become the head of A&R at Columbia without an eye for a market, and the selections on the *Sing Along* albums were far from random. Before

going into the studio to record *Still More Sing Along*, Mitch Miller had intensively researched among Boy and Girl Scout groups, Rotarian clubs, and similar organizations, consulting then on the kinds of songs they most enjoyed.

Armed with this information Miller prepared a selection that ranged from the unashamedly sentimental to the relentlessly cheery. The result was another hit, another gold record and an album that remained on the charts for 78 weeks, peaking at Number Four.

1 **In A Shanty In Old Shanty Town** (2:51)
2 **Smiles** (2:37)
3 **I'll Be With You In Apple Blossom Time** (2:40)
4 **Memories** (2:42)
5 **When Day Is Done** (3:49)
6 **Good Night, Sweetheart** (2:52)
7 **Tip-toe Through The Tulips With Me** (2:20)
8 **Medley: A Bicycle Built For Two/Put On Your Old Grey Bonnet** (2:09)
9 **Medley: The Band Played On/Oh! You Beautiful Doll** (2:32)
10 **Medley: Hinky Dinky Parlez-Vous/She'll Be Comin' Round The Mountain** (2:28)
11 **Beer Barrel Polka** (2:58)
12 **Medley: When Your Sweet Sixteen/Silver Threads Among The Gold** (3:41)

Total album length: 36 minutes

Number One singles:
None

Grammy awards:
None

Label: US: Columbia

Recorded in: New York, USA

Personnel:
Mitch Miller And The Gang
Jimmy Carroll

Producer:
Mitch Miller

STILL MORE!

(Includes special sing-along lyric sheets)

COLUMBIA GUARANTEED HIGH FIDELITY · LP

SING ALONG WITH MITCH

Mitch Miller & the Gang · WHEN YOU WERE SWEET SIXTEEN
TIP-TOE THRU THE TULIPS WITH ME · WHEN DAY IS DONE
BEER BARREL POLKA · IN A SHANTY IN OLD SHANTY TOWN
HINKY DINKY PARLEZ-VOUS · A BICYCLE BUILT FOR TWO
SMILES ★ I'LL BE WITH YOU IN APPLE BLOSSOM TIME
PUT ON YOUR OLD GREY BONNET ★ GOOD NIGHT, SWEETHEART
OH! YOU BEAUTIFUL DOLL · I'M JUST WILD ABOUT MARY
SHE'LL BE COMING 'ROUND THE MOUNTAIN · MEMORIES
THE BAND PLAYED ON · SILVER THREADS AMONG THE GOLD

CL 1283

41 Open Fire, Two Guitars

| • **Album sales:** 500,000 | • **Highest position:** 4 | • **Release date:** 1959 |

Mitch Miller, the 1950s music business svengali and the man behind Johnny Mathis' career, was not someone known for taking risks, which makes it all the more surprising that this, Mathis' eighth album in little more than two years, should have come as such a contrast to what had gone before.

Mathis' previous album, *Swing Softly,* had been a big band affair, orchestrated by Percy Faith. *Open Fire, Two Guitars*, by contrast, was just as simple as its title suggests. Mathis went into the studio accompanied almost exclusively by two ace guitarists, Al Caiola and Tony Mottola, the sound being unobtrusively filled out by a subtle bass (mostly provided by jazz-legend turned CBS-studio mainman Milt Hinton).

When it came to the choice of songs, however, Miller and Mathis stayed with their usual formula of show tunes, standards and a sprinkling of tasteful originals. Highlights include the title track, an uncharacteristically romantic piece from Leiber and Stoller, and a delicate reading of 'In The Still Of The Night'.

The result was an album that is an enduring favourite among Mathis fans, one that remained in the charts for a remarkable 74 weeks, peaking at Number Four and going gold along the way.

Number One singles:
None

Grammy awards: None

Label: US: Columbia:
UK: Fontana

Recorded in: New York,
USA

Personnel:
Johnny Mathis
Al Caiola
Tony Mottola
Milt Hinton
Frank Carroll

Producer:
Mitch Miller

1 **Open Fire** (3:52)
2 **Bye Bye Blackbird** (4:07)
3 **In The Still Of The Night** (2:35)
4 **Embraceable You** (3:28)
5 **I'll Be Seeing You** (4:26)
6 **Tenderly** (2:58)
7 **When I Fall In Love** (4:31)
8 **I Concentrate On You** (3:16)
9 **Please Be Kind** (3:24)
10 **You'll Never Know** (4:07)
11 **I'm Just A Boy In Love** (2:44)
12 **My Funny Valentine** (3:37)

Total album length: 43 minutes

Open Fire, Two Guitars

JOHNNY MATHIS

Fontana

Tenderly · Open Fire · I Concentrate on You · In the Still of the Night
I'll Be Seeing You · I'm Just a Boy in Love · You'll Never Know
Please Be Kind · Embraceable You · My Funny Valentine
When I Fall in Love · Bye Bye Blackbird

© FONTANA Printed in England

40 Tchaikovsky 1812

| • **Album sales:** 500,000 | • **Highest position:** 3 | • **Release date:** March 1959 |

The Hungarian conductor Antal Dorati's interpretation of Tchaikovsky's 1812 is a landmark in classical music recording. The 1950s was a time of enormous progress in recording technology and Mercury Records, with their Mercury Living Presence Series, particularly aimed at hi-fi enthusiasts, had been in the forefront of these advances.

Mercury's pre-eminence in this area was largely down to the husband-and-wife team of Bob Fine and Wilma Cozart Fine. Bob Fine was an inventor who devised a three microphone scheme for recording an orchestra. Wilma had the complex job of mixing the three tracks down to two stereo tracks. Tchaikovsky's 1812 offered a perfect chance to show off their skills. In the interest of verisimilitude they even used an authentic 18th-century cannon and a genuine cathedral carillon in the recording.

Antal Dorati – by this time a US citizen working with the Minneapolis Symphony Orchestra and the University of Minnesota Brass Band – was the favoured conductor for the Mercury team. The result was a milestone in recorded sound, an album that stands to this day as a definitive recording of the work. It proved a big hit with both classical music lovers and hi-fi buffs and went to Number Three in the charts, soon earning a gold record.

Number One singles:
None

Grammy awards:
None

Label: US: Mercury

Recorded in: N/A

Personnel:
Antal Dorati (d. 1988)
Minneapolis Symphony
  Orchestra
University of Minnesota
  Brass Band

Producer:
Wilma Cozart Fine

1   **1812 Festival Overture, Op.49**
2   **Capriccio Italien, Op.45**

Official times not available

TCHAIKOVSKY

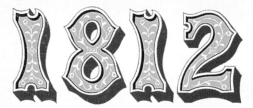

FESTIVAL OVERTURE, Op. 49
(ORIGINAL SCORING)

CAPRICCIO ITALIEN

ANTAL DORATI
Minneapolis Symphony Orchestra
University of Minnesota BRASS BAND
18TH CENTURY FRENCH BRONZE CANNON
COURTESY U.S. MILITARY ACADEMY, WEST POINT, NEW YORK

BELLS of Giant Carillon
Spoken Commentary by DEEMS TAYLOR

...rd Corporation, 35 E. Wacker Drive, Chicago, Illinois 60601 • Printed in U.S.A.

39 …From The Hungry I

• **Album sales:** 500,000 | • **Highest position:** 2 (less than 1 week) | • **Release date:** January 1959 |

The Kingston Trio's second album found them in a highly unusual situation. When they recorded it live at a San Francisco club in the summer of 1958 they were just another popular club and college folk act. By the time it was released they were the hottest group in the country. The transformation had come about because of the huge success of the folk song 'Tom Dooley', a single from their debut album. All of a sudden the Trio had become famous.

If The Kingston Trio had known what was in store, perhaps this second album would have been a more self-conscious affair. Instead it preserved for posterity the easygoing charm of the Trio's live act. The songs come from all over the world. There's a French lullaby in 'Gue Gue Gue', a Trinidadian Calypso in 'Zombie Jamboree', a South African folk song in 'Wimoweh' and an Appalachian one in 'Shady Grove'. As much as the songs themselves, though, it's the on-stage banter that really conveys the Trio's particular live appeal.

Despite the lack of a hit single *From The Hungry I* spent 47 weeks on the charts, peaking at Number Two and earning a gold record. The Kingston Trio are still playing to sold out audiences today and garnering rave reviews wherever they go. The trio now consists of original member Bob Shane plus George Grove and Bobby Haworth.

Number One singles:
None

Grammy awards:
None

Label: US: Capitol

Recorded in: San Francisco, USA

Personnel:
Bob Shane
Nick Reynolds
Dave Guard

Producer:
Voyle Gilmore

1   Tic, Tic (2:12)
2   Gue, Gue, Gue (2:52)
3   Dorie (2:59)
4   South Coast (4:28)
5   Zombie Jamboree (3:16)
6   Wimoweh (Mbube) (2:46)
7   New York Girls (2:36)
8   They Call The Wind Maria (4:48)
9   Merry Minuet (2:26)
10 Shady Grove/Lonesome Traveler (3:31)
11 When The Saints Go Marching In (3:43)

Total album length: 36 minutes

The Kingston Trio

...from the "Hungry i"

The Kingston Trio

RECORDED IN LIVE PERFORMANCE

Capitol RECORDS

HIGH FIDELITY RECORDING

38 Belafonte at Carnegie Hall

• **Album sales:** 500,000 │ • **Highest position:** 2 (less than 1 week) │ • **Release date:** November 1959 │

This live album was taken from two performances by Harry Belafonte as he entertained a huge audience at Carnegie Hall at the height of his career. It was a milestone in recording history, being one of the first live music albums to become a bestseller and showcasing Belafonte's sparkling talent as a concert performer. The concert focused on three main areas of music: the first section was called 'Moods Of The American Negro', the second 'In The Caribbean' and the third, 'Around the World'.

The spontaneous, relaxed atmosphere that Belafonte created depended on the highly professional musical direction of producer Bob Bollard. Backing the singer was a 47-piece orchestra led by Bob Corman, as well as a small group of two guitars, bass and percussion. Opening with Leadbelly's 'Cotton Fields', Belafonte sang his way through all his major hits, such as 'The Banana Boat Song (Day-O)' and 'Jamaica Farewell'. Belafonte's version of 'Matilda', at just under 12 minutes, was one of the longest live versions recorded and featured a great deal of audience participation, another unusual and rewarding aspect of the album.

Released in 1959, the album reached Number Two on the charts and continued to be a bestseller for three more years.

Number One singles:
None

Grammy awards:
Best engineering
contribution other than
classical or novelty

Label: US: RCA

Recorded in: New York, USA

Personnel:
Harry Belafonte
Bob Corman and
  orchestra

Producer:
Bob Bollard

1   **Introduction/Darlin' Cora (3:59)**
2   **Sylvie (4:54)**
3   **Cotton Fields (4:18)**
4   **John Henry (5:11)**
5   **Marching Saints (2:50)**
6   **Banana Boat Song (Day-O) (3:40)**
7   **Jamaica Farewell (5:10)**
8   **Mama Look a Boo Boo (5:24)**
9   **Come Back Liza (3:06)**
10 **Man Smart (Woman Smarter) (4:23)**
11 **Hava Nagila (4:03)**
12 **Danny Boy (5:21)**
13 **Cucurrucuca Paloma (3:50)**
14 **Shenandoah (3:48)**
15 **Matilda (11:27)**

Total album length: 71 minutes

BELAFONTE
AT CARNEGIE HALL

LIVING·STEREO

RCA

33⅓ R.P.M

SF-5050

"Stereo Orthophonic" High Fidelity Recording

37 Songs For Swingin' Lovers!

| • **Album sales:** 500,000 | • **Highest position:** 2 (1 week) | • **Release date:** 1956 |

Sinatra's first album for Hollywood's Capitol Records, *In The Wee Small Hours*, had effectively re-ignited his recording career. No longer the teen idol of the 1940s, Sinatra was now presented as the lonesome, world-weary crooner. It would have been easy to follow up with more of the same, but Sinatra and his arranger, Nelson Riddle, had a better idea: they decided to balance the downtempo pathos of the previous album with something defiantly uptempo and swinging. It was a formula Sinatra was to stick to for many years to come.

Songs For Swingin' Lovers! set the template for Sinatra's run of uptempo albums. The songs were mostly well-seasoned pop standards and songs from musical theatre. Riddle set up a solid rhythm section and created subtle string arrangements, leaving plenty of room for Sinatra to stamp his personality over them.

From the opening 'You Make Me Feel So Young' through to the Cole Porter classic 'I've Got You Under My Skin', this album set the standard for popular singers of the period. It was an immediate hit with the public too, reaching Number Two on the US charts where it remained for 50 weeks, and becoming Sinatra's first album to earn a gold disc.

Number One singles:
None

Grammy awards:
None

Label: US: Capitol

Recorded in: Hollywood, USA

Personnel:
Frank Sinatra (d. 1998)
Nelson Riddle

Producer:
Voyle Gilmore

1   **You Make Me Feel So Young (2:57)**
2   **It Happened In Monterey (2:36)**
3   **You're Getting To Be A Habit With Me (2:19)**
4   **You Brought A New Kind Of Love To Me (2:48)**
5   **Too Marvelous For Words (2:29)**
6   **Old Devil Moon (3:56)**
7   **Pennies From Heaven (2:44)**
8   **Love Is Here To Stay (2:42)**
9   **I've Got You Under My Skin (3:43)**
10 **I Thought About You (2:30)**
11 **We'll Be Together Again (4:26)**
12 **Makin' Whoopee (3:06)**
13 **Swingin' Down The Lane (2:54)**
14 **Anything Goes (2:43)**
15 **How About You? (2:45)**

Total album length: 45 minutes

Frank Sinatra

songs for Swingin' lovers!

YOU MAKE ME FEEL SO YOUNG • IT HAPPENED IN MONTEREY • YOU'RE GETTING TO BE A HABIT WITH ME • YOU BROUGHT A NEW KIND OF LOVE
TO ME • TOO MARVELOUS FOR WORDS • OLD DEVIL MOON • PENNIES FROM HEAVEN • LOVE IS HERE TO STAY • I'VE GOT YOU UNDER MY SKIN •
I THOUGHT ABOUT YOU • WE'LL BE TOGETHER AGAIN • MAKIN' WHOOPEE • SWINGIN' DOWN THE LANE • ANYTHING GOES • HOW ABOUT YOU ?

36 Warm

| • **Album sales:** 500,000 | • **Highest position:** 2 (4 weeks) | • **Release date:** November 1957 |

In 1957, Columbia was under the direction of easy-listening supremo Mitch Miller, who established the formula that made Johnny Mathis the pre-eminent albums artist of the late 1950s. *Warm* followed on from Mathis' breakthrough album *Wonderful, Wonderful*, retaining the same arranger, Percy Faith, as well as his orchestra. *Warm*'s sound was as intimate, romantic and gentle as the title suggests.

What made Mathis' albums unusual for their time was that, rather than function simply as collections featuring a couple of hit singles surrounded by filler, they went in the opposite direction and didn't feature his hit singles at all. This strategy later paid off when Mathis' first *Greatest Hits* collection became a huge chart success. Instead, the Mathis albums concentrated on building up a lush romantic mood with a sophisticated mix of show tunes, standards, and ballads. On this album, there are selections from such well-known songwriters Irving Berlin ('What'll I Do') and Lerner and Loewe ('I've Grown Accustomed To Her Face'), as well as a number of lesser-known tunes.

Warm spent an impressive 50 weeks on the album charts, with four weeks at Number Two, and was Mathis' first album to go gold.

Number One singles:
None

Grammy awards:
None

Label: US: Columbia;
UK: Fontana

Recorded: New York, USA

Personnel:
Johnny Mathis
Percy Faith & His
    Orchestra

Producer:
Mitch Miller
Don Law

1   **Warm** (3:26)
2   **My One And Only Love** (3:40)
3   **Baby, Baby, Baby** (3:03)
4   **A Handful Of Stars** (3:23)
5   **By Myself** (4:11)
6   **I've Grown Accustomed To Her Face** (3:32)
7   **Then I'll Be Tired Of You** (4:10)
8   **I'm Glad There Is You** (4:07)
9   **What'll I Do?** (2:58)
10 **The Lovely Things You Do** (3:21)
11 **There Goes My Heart** (3:43)
12 **While We're Young** (2:44)

Total album length: 42 minutes

Johnny Mathis

JOHNNY MATHIS

PERCY FAITH AND HIS ORCHESTRA

fontana

WARM

35 Come Dance With Me!

• **Album sales:** 500,000 │ • **Highest position:** 2 (5 weeks) │ • **Release date:** 1959 │

There was only one way for Frank Sinatra to follow-up the supremely heartbroken *Only The Lonely* and that was with an upbeat antidote, following his now established pattern of alternating fast and slow albums.

Come Dance With Me was a companion piece to the previous year's uptempo hit 'Come Fly With Me'. For this new album, despite Nelson Riddle's sterling work on *Only The Lonely*, Sinatra decided to team up once again with arranger Billy May, whose hard-driving style had made *Come Fly With Me* such a roaring success.

May certainly came up trumps. The album is considered to be Sinatra's hardest-swinging set of songs, with a horn section that sounds punchier than ever. The album won the award for Best Vocal Album Of The Year at the newly established Grammy awards, and Sinatra received a second Grammy for Best Vocal Performance for his work on Van Heusen and Cahn's title track. Other critical successes included his definitive takes on 'Just In Time' and Irving Berlin's 'Cheek To Cheek'.

Come Dance With Me comfortably extended Sinatra's run of hit albums. It reached Number Two in the charts, stayed there for exactly a year going gold along the way.

Number One singles:
None

Grammy awards: Album of the year, Best vocal performance, male – Come Dance With Me

Label: US: Capitol

Recorded in: Hollywood, USA

Personnel:
Frank Sinatra (d. 1998)
Billy May And His Orchestra

Producer:
Dave Cavanaugh

1   **Come Dance With Me** (2:31)
2   **Something's Gotta Give** (2:38)
3   **Just In Time** (2:24)
4   **Dancing In The Dark** (2:26)
5   **Too Close For Comfort** (2:34)
6   **I Could Have Danced All Night** (2:40)
7   **Saturday Night** (1:54)
8   **Day In-Day Out** (3:25)
9   **Cheek To Cheek** (3:06)
10 **Baubles, Bangles And Beads** (2:46)
11 **The Song Is You** (2:43)
12 **The Last Dance** (2:11)

Total album length: 32 minutes

Frank Sinatra

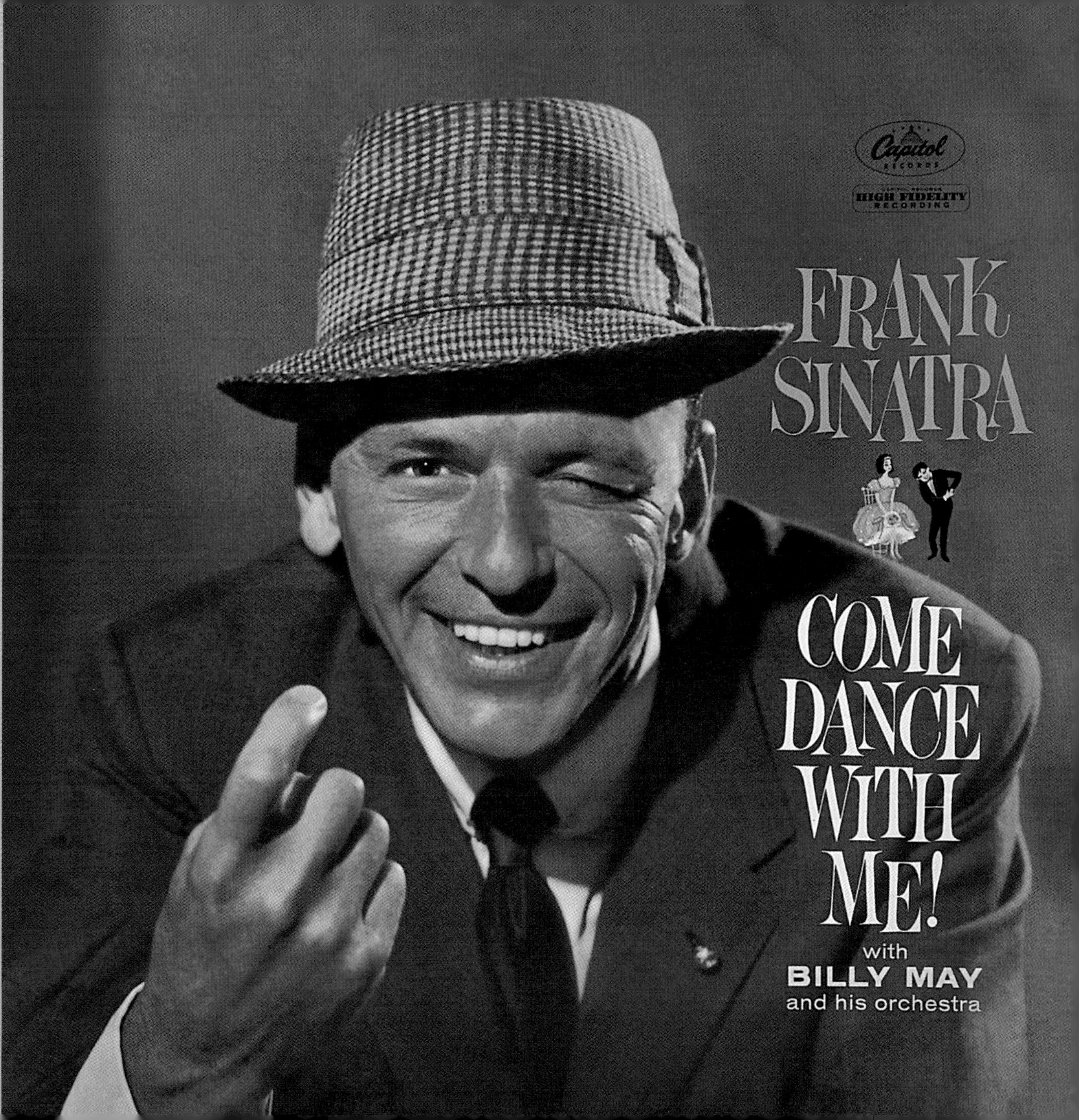

Capitol
RECORDS
HIGH FIDELITY
RECORDING
FRANK SINATRA
COME DANCE WITH ME!
with
BILLY MAY
and his orchestra

34 An Evening With Belafonte

| • **Album sales:** 500,000 | • **Highest position:** 2 (6 weeks) | • **Release date:** March 1957 |

After presenting a set of West Indian songs on his bestselling album *Calypso*, Harry Belafonte went back to the varied folk influences of his earlier career. *An Evening With Belafonte* is a selection of songs from all around the world – an early example of today's 'world music'.

The album opens with a song from Haiti ('Merci, Bon Dieu') and travels from Israel ('Hava Nageela') and Mexico ('Cu Cu Ru Cu Cu Paloma'), taking in songs from the US and Europe along the way. The traditional material includes songs such as 'Come O My Love', 'Shenandoah' and 'When the Saints Go Marching In'. Other songs, such as 'Eden Was Just Like This' by Irving Burgie (Lord Burgess), were written in an ethnic style. Belafonte also recorded the well-known 'Danny Boy', a song based on the Irish tune, the 'Londonderry Air'.

Although Belafonte would never score with a single as big as 'Day O' the biggest success of the album was once again West Indian: the Christmas song 'Mary's Boy Child' became a seasonal hit and sold especially well in the UK.

Although the album was not as massive a hit as *Calypso*, it sold well, and helped establish Belafonte's reputation as a cosmopolitan artist at home with music from many different cultures. It was becoming apparent that Harry Belafonte was not so much interested in hit singles as he was in providing miniature lessons in global folk music.

Number One singles:
None

Grammy awards:
None

Label: US & UK: RCA

Recorded in: Hollywood, USA

Personnel:
Harry Belafonte
Will Lorin and his
   Orchestra
Millard J. Thomas
Frantz Casseus

Producers:
Henri René
Dennis Farnon
EO Welker

1 Merci, Bon Dieu (2:49)
2 Once Was (4:45)
3 Hava Nageela (3:13)
4 Danny Boy (5:50)
5 The Drummer And The Cook (3:55)
6 Come O My Love (4:26)
7 Shenandoah (3:45)
8 Mary's Boy Child (4:20)
9 Cu Cu Ru Cu Cu Paloma (5:30)
10 Eden Was Just Like This (2:59)
11 When The Saints Go Marching In (3:39)

Total album length: 45 minutes

RCA

33⅓ R.P.M
RD 27001
A "New Orthophonic" High Fidelity Recording

An
Evening
with
Belafonte

33 The King And I

| • Album sales: 500,000 | • Highest position: 1 (1 week) | • Release date: 1956 |

On its release in 1956, the soundtrack album of *The King and I* reflected the immense popularity of the film, which starred Yul Brynner and Deborah Kerr. For the film, Brynner sang his own songs, but Kerr's were dubbed by Marni Nixon, who was also the voice behind Audrey Hepburn in *My Fair Lady*.

Set in the 1860s, the story revolves around Anna, a young woman who travels to Bangkok as a governess to teach King Mongkut's children, and ends up falling in love with her employer. The period and the exotic setting made for a lavish on-screen production, backed up musically on the soundtrack by Alfred Newman's large studio orchestra playing a score with grand-scale orchestrations and sweeping string arrangements. Marni Nixon, one of the most highly respected singers in musical theatre, gave impressive performances of the female lead numbers 'I Whistle A Happy Tune', 'Hello, Young Lovers' and 'Getting To Know You', with Deborah Kerr taking the speaking parts. Yul Brynner and Marni Nixon's version of 'Shall We Dance?' was also considered a huge success.

Number One singles:
None

Grammy awards:
None

Label: US: Capitol

Recorded in: California, USA

Producer: N/A

Personnel:
Marni Nixon
Yul Brynner (d. 1985)
Leona Gordon
Reuben Fuentes
Terry Saunders
Robert Russell Bennett
Ken Darby
Gus Levene
Edward B. Powell
Alfred Newman
Twentieth Century Fox Orchestra

1 Main Title (1:40)
2 I Whistle A Happy Tune (2:41)
3 My Lord And Master (2:10)
4 March Of The Siamese Children (3:23)
5 Anna And The Royal Wives (2:29)
6 Hello, Young Lovers (3:28)
7 A Puzzlement (3:27)
8 Getting To Know You (5:00)
9 Garden Rendezvous (2:31)
10 We Kiss In A Shadow (2:38)
11 I Have Dreamed (3:36)
12 Shall I Tell You What I Think of You? (3:37)
13 Something Wonderful (3:09)
14 Prayer To Buddha (2:16)
15 Waltz Of Anna And Sir Edward (1:40)
16 The Small House Of Uncle Thomas (12:57)
17 Song Of The King (1:32)
18 Shall We Dance? (4:22)
19 The Letter (3:02)
20 Something Wonderful (Finale) (3:11)
21 Overture (6:36)

Total album length: 75 minutes

Original Soundtrack

FROM THE SOUND TRACK OF THE MOTION PICTURE
RODGERS AND HAMMERSTEIN'S
The King and I
A 20TH CENTURY-FOX CINEMASCOPE 55 PICTURE
Capitol RECORDS
CAPITOL RECORDS HIGH FIDELITY RECORDING

32 Film Encores

| • **Album sales:** 500,000 | • **Highest position:** 1 (1 week) | • **Release date:** May 1957 |

By the time *Film Encores* was released, in the spring of 1957, Mantovani was established firmly as America's favourite orchestral conductor. A successful tour of the US in late 1956, ending at New York's Carnegie Hall, had raised his profile considerably, but it was as a recording artist he excelled. He had enjoyed hit records since the 1930s, but the new album format of the 1950s was ideally suited to light classical music. Mantovani capitalised on this, becoming one of the first musicians to specialise in recorded, rather than live, performance.

Film Encores was effectively a sequel to his 1955 hit album *Song Hits For Theatreland,* this time swapping screen for stage. It's a collection that concentrates, unsurprisingly, on grand romantic melodies, never more so than with the opening trio of 'My Foolish Heart', 'Unchained

Melody' and 'Over The Rainbow'. There is also some uptempo variation later on, with the inclusion of such tracks as 'High Noon' and 'Hi-Lili Hi-Lo'. Throughout the album, Mantovani's trademark 'cascading strings', as developed with arranger Ronald Binge, are featured. This was precisely the kind of sophisticated easy listening that those Americans able to afford hi-fi systems and LPs in the mid-1950s were looking for.

Film Encores was Mantovani's one and only Number One album. It remained on the charts for more than two years and earned him a gold disc.

Number One singles:
None

Grammy Awards:
None

Label: US & UK: Decca

Recorded in: N/A

Personnel:
Mantovani (d. 1980)

Producer: N/A

1 **My Foolish Heart**
2 **Unchained Melody**
3 **Over The Rainbow**
4 **Summertime In Venice**
5 **Intermezzo**
6 **Three Coins in the Fountain**
7 **Love is a Many-Splendored Thing**
8 **Laura**
9 **High Noon**
10 **Hi-Lili Hi-Lo**
11 **September Song**
12 **Theme From Limelight**

Official times not available

Mantovani

Mantovani
Film Encores

Mantovani
and his orchestra

DECCA
RECORDS

LK 4200

31 Merry Christmas

• **Album sales:** 500,000 | • **Highest position:** 1 (1 week) | • **Release date:** December 1957 |

The 1950s was a decade in which the Christmas album reigned supreme. All the major artists of the day recorded one, but the undisputed king of the Christmas record was Bing Crosby. His 'White Christmas', written by Irving Berlin and originally recorded in just 18 minutes back in 1942, is the most successful Christmas single ever made, and has since sold over 30,000,000 copies.

Naturally enough, given his success, Crosby was quick to release a Christmas album. His *Merry Christmas* collection was originally released in 1945 with 10 songs spread over a set of five 78rpm discs. It was then re-released in 1949 as a 10-inch album, this time featuring eight songs. Finally, with the advent of the 12-inch long-playing album in 1955, it was released in its definitive form with 12 songs. Among

others, the Irish-themed 'Christmas In Killarney' and the Hawaiian 'Mele Kalikimaka' were added.

Support for Bing came from fellow wartime stars, The Andrews Sisters, who appear on 'Jingle Bells' and 'Santa Claus is Comin' to Town'. *Merry Christmas* didn't show up in the Billboard charts until 1957, but then it reached Number One in the charts and returned every year until 1962, going gold in the process.

Number One singles:	Recorded in: N/A
None	
	Personnel:
Grammy awards: None	Bing Crosby (d. 1977)
	The Andrews Sisters
Label: US: Decca:	
UK: Brunswick	Producer: N/A

1 **Silent Night** (2:39)
2 **Adeste Fideles** (3:12)
3 **White Christmas** (3:04)
4 **God Rest Ye Merry Gentlemen** (2:18)
5 **Faith Of Our Fathers** (2:54)
6 **I'll Be Home For Christmas** (2:56)
7 **Jingle Bells** (2:36)
8 **Santa Claus Is Comin' To Town** (2:42)
9 **Silver Bells** (3:04)
10 **It's Beginning To Look Like Christmas** (2:49)
11 **Christmas In Killarney** (2:44)
12 **Mele Kalikimaka** (2:55)

Total album length: 34 minutes

Bing Crosby

mono LAT 8556

Brunswick

Merry Christmas

Adeste Fidelis • I'll Be Home for Christmas • White Christmas • God Rest Ye Merry, Gentlemen • It's Beginning to Look Like Christmas
Silent Night • Jingle Bells (with the Andrews Sisters) • Christmas in Killarney • Santa Claus is Comin' to Town (with the Andrews Sisters)
Faith of Our Fathers • Silver Bells (with Carole Richards) • Mele Kalikimaka (Merry Christmas) (with the Andrews Sisters)

30 The Kingston Trio

| • **Album sales:** 500,000 | • **Highest position:** 1 (1 week) | • **Release date:** June 1958 |

The Kingston Trio's first album was one of those rare records that are released with little fanfare or expectation, but go on to be a huge success, changing the entire musical landscape. *Kingston Trio* was the record that ignited the folk music boom of the late-1950s and early-1960s.

The group, a trio of Californian college friends, had been spotted by agent Jimmy Saphier in the summer of 1957 while playing a residency at San Francisco's Purple Onion Club. Capitol Records then signed them up and sent them into the studio with Frank Sinatra's producer, Voyle Gilmore, to record their debut album.

Three days in the making, the album offered a fairly straight reflection of their stage show. It included traditional folk songs ('Three Jolly Coachmen', 'Saro Jane'), calypsos ('Banua', 'Santo Anno') and contemporary folk songs like Tom Gillkyson's 'Fast Freight'. Above all, though, it contained an insidiously catchy murder ballad called 'Tom Dooley'. Released as a single, 'Tom Dooley' became an enormous hit, selling over 3,000,000 copies and pulling the album along in its wake. When 'Tom Dooley' went gold in 1958, the folk revival was born, setting the stage for Bob Dylan, Joan Baez, The Byrds and Peter, Paul & Mary, and the protest movement of the 1960s.

The album hit Number One and spent well over two years on the album charts.

Number One singles:
US: Tom Dooley

Grammy awards:
Best country & western
performance – Tom
Dooley

Label: US: Capitol

Recorded in: Hollywood,
USA

Personnel:
Bob Shane
Nick Reynolds
Dave Guard

Producer:
Voyle Gilmore

1 **Three Jolly Coachmen (1:47)**
2 **Bay of Mexico (2:52)**
3 **Banua (1:37)**
4 **Tom Dooley (3:03)**
5 **Fast Freight (3:48)**
6 **Hard, Ain't It Hard (2:24)**
7 **Saro Jane (2:24)**
8 **Sloop John (3:31)**
9 **Santo Anno (2:17)**
10 **Scotch and Soda (2:33)**
11 **Coplas (2:38)**
12 **Little Maggie (1:48)**

Total album length: 31 minutes

THE KINGSTON TRIO

29 The Lord's Prayer

| • **Album sales:** 500,000 | • **Highest position:** 1 (1 week) | • **Release date:** September 1959 |

The Mormon Tabernacle Choir may have been one of the more unlikely groups to top the album charts, but they were certainly the longest established. The choir had originally been formed in 1847 while the tabernacle itself, with its mighty organ, was built 20 years later. By the late 1950s the Choir's music became familiar to millions. Their weekly radio show *Music and the Spoken Word*, had begun in 1932 and it still continues today – the longest uninterrupted network broadcast in American radio history.

The Mormon Tabernacle Choir's first long-playing record was released as far back as 1949 but it was a decade before they crossed over into the charts. By then religious music was no longer unknown to the commercial record buyer – Tennessee Ernie Ford had sold millions of his devotional records – but the huge sound of the choir, backed by a newly rebuilt organ that now boasted 11,000 pipes, was something new.

The sheer power of the choir's sound, particularly on the Grammy-winning rendition of the 'Battle Hymn Of The Republic', was enough to persuade the public to go out and buy the album in quantities sufficient to take it all the way to the Number One spot and in the process earn *The Lord's Prayer* a gold record.

Number One singles:
None

Grammy awards: Best vocal group/chorus – Battle Hymn Of The Republic

Label: US: Columbia

Recorded in: Salt Lake City, USA

Personnel:
The Mormon Tabernacle Choir
Dr. Richard P. Condie
The Philadelphia Orchestra
Eugene Ormandy
Alexander Schriener
Frank W. Asper

Producer: N/A

1 **The Lord's Prayer**
2 **Come, Come Ye Saints**
3 **Blessed Are They That Mourn**
4 **O, My Father Side**
5 **How Great The Wisdom And The Love**
6 **Holy, Holy, Holy**
7 **148th Psalm**
8 **For Unto Us A Child Is Born**
9 **David's Lamentation**
10 **Londonderry Air**
11 **Battle Hymn Of The Republic**

Official times not available

The Mormon Tabernacle Choir

THE LORD'S PRAYER

THE MORMON TABERNACLE CHOIR
THE PHILADELPHIA ORCHESTRA, EUGENE ORMANDY

PHOTO: W. LEE ® Columbia Masterworks Marcas Reg. Printed in U.S.A.

28 Christmas Sing-Along With Mitch

| • **Album sales:** 500,000 | • **Highest position:** 1 (2 weeks) | • **Release date:** 1958 |

Perhaps the best loved of the whole *Sing Along* series and the second-best selling on its original release, *Christmas Sing-Along With Mitch* once more gave the public exactly what they were looking for.However, the album wasn't exactly what one might have expected from such an unashamedly commercial series (one that was in effect the karaoke substitute of its day). There's no 'Jingle Bells' here. Instead this is an entirely religious selection – one devoted to Christmas rather than Xmas.

Miller's background in light orchestral work is rather more apparent in this volume of the series than elsewhere, as he adapts the likes of 'Adeste Fideles' and 'Silent Night'. There are also, for the first time in the series, some *a cappella* selections, including the 'Coventry Carol'.

Overall the tone is reverent rather than party-oriented. Miller would make up for that a couple of years later by recording *Holiday Sing Along*, with Santa songs in abundance. But for the Christmas of 1959 he evidently read the mood of the American people right: *Christmas Sing Along* went straight to Number One, earned a gold record, and duly reappeared in the charts each Christmas for the next five years.

| **Number One singles:** | **Recorded in:** New York, |
| None | USA |

| **Grammy awards:** | **Personnel:** |
| None | Mitch Miller And The Gang |

| **Label:** US: Columbia | **Producer:** |
| | Mitch Miller |

1   Joy To The World (3:54)
2   Hark! The Herald Angels Sing (2:05)
3   What Child Is This? (Greensleeves) (3:26)
4   We Three Kings Of Orient Are (2:24)
5   It Came Upon A Midnight Clear (3:51)
6   Silent Night (1:46)
7   Deck The Hall With Boughs Of Holly (1:52)
8   God Rest Ye Merry, Gentlemen (2:26)
9   O Come All Ye Faithful (4:23)
10 The First Noel (2:05)
11 The Coventry Carol (2:52)
12 O Little Town Of Bethlehem (3:01)

Total album length: 34 minutes

CS 8027

STEREO  FIDELITY

 GUARANTEED HIGH FIDELITY

CHRISTMAS
SING-ALONG WITH MITCH

PHOTO OF MITCHELL JR., MARGARET, FRAN AND MITCH MILLER

PHOTO: BOB CATO

MITCH MILLER & THE GANG

JOY TO THE WORLD HARK! THE HERALD ANGELS SING
WHAT CHILD IS THIS (Greensleeves) WE THREE KINGS
IT CAME UPON THE MIDNIGHT CLEAR SILENT NIGHT
DECK THE HALL GOD REST YE MERRY, GENTLEMEN
O COME, ALL YE FAITHFUL THE FIRST NOEL
THE COVENTRY CAROL ★ AWAY IN A MANGER
O LITTLE TOWN OF BETHLEHEM (Includes special sing-along lyric sheets)

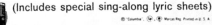

Flower Drum Song

| • **Album sales:** 500,000 | • **Highest position:** 1 (3 weeks) | • **Release date:** 1958 |

The album of *Flower Drum Song* was released in 1958, after a run of over 600 performances as a Broadway show. Here, Rodgers and Hammerstein explore the generation gap in the context of San Francisco's Chinatown. The story centres around nightclub-owner Sammy Fong, whose family order him a bride from China. In the ensuing drama, issues of cultural difference and assimilation are aired lightheartedly, in songs such as 'A Hundred Million Miracles', sung by Miyoshi Umeki in the role of Mei Li, and 'Don't Marry Me', sung by Larry Blydon as Sammy Fong.

The romantic numbers (such as 'You Are Beautiful' and 'Love, Look Away') are also highlights of the show, though they have proved less popular over time than the frequently covered comic number 'I Enjoy Being A Girl', sung by Pat Suzuki as Linda Low. Suzuki's assertive, brash performance as Low, an Americanized nightclub dancer, contrasted strongly with the Umeki's as Mei Li, the shy young woman newly arrived in the West, pointing up the differences between the two cultures.

The musical was widely acclaimed, but less so than Rodgers and Hammerstein's other productions, possibly because it appeared in the same year as *West Side Story*.

Number One singles:
None

Grammy awards:
None

Label: US: Columbia;
UK: Philips

Recorded in: N/A

Personnel:
Miyoshi Umeki
Larry Blyden
Pat Suzuki
Juanita Hall
Ed Kenney
Arabella Hong
Keye Luke

Producer:
Goddard Lieberson

1   **Overture** (4:13)
2   **You Are Beautiful** (4:04)
3   **A Hundred Million Miracles** (4:26)
4   **I Enjoy Being A Girl** (3:37)
5   **I Am Going To Like It Here** (3:53)
6   **Like A God** (1:36)
7   **Chop Suey** (2:39)
8   **Don't Marry Me** (4:13)
9   **Grant Avenue** (2:36)
10 **Love, Look Away** (3:35)
11 **At The Celestial Bar: Fan Tan Fannie** (5:06)
12 **Entr'acte** (1:34)
13 **The Other Generation** (3:17)
14 **Sunday** (4:23)
15 **The Other Generation (Reprise)** (2:03)

Total album length: 51 minutes

RODGERS & HAMMERSTEIN in association with JOSEPH FIELDS
present a New Musical

FLOWER DRUM SONG

Music by
RICHARD RODGERS

Lyrics by
OSCAR HAMMERSTEIN 2nd

Book by
OSCAR HAMMERSTEIN 2nd and **JOSEPH FIELDS**

Based on the novel by **C. Y. Lee**

with
Miyoshi Umeki

Larry Blyden

Juanita Hall • Ed Kenney

Keye Luke • Arabella Hong

and
Pat Suzuki

Directed by
GENE KELLY

Choreography by
Carol Haney
Scenery by
Oliver Smith
Costumes by
Irene Sharaff
Lighting by
Peggy Clark
Orchestrations by
Robert Russell Bennett
Musical Director
Salvatore Dell'Isola
Dance Arrangements by
Luther Henderson, Jr.
Produced for records by
Goddard Lieberson

PHILIPS

HI-FI-STEREO

26 Elvis

| • **Album sales:** 500,000 | • **Highest position:** 1 (5 weeks) | • **Release date:** November 1956 |

Elvis' second album was recorded little more than six months after his debut, but his career had changed utterly in the interim. Those six months had seen Elvis become the hottest new star in America, a symbol of cultural degeneracy to some but an idol to many more.

With one exception (the Arthur Crudup blues-number 'So Glad You're Mine' (which was left over from Elvis' first-ever RCA session) the album was recorded in three days in Hollywood, using Elvis' regular band, augmented this time by Dudley Brooks' piano playing and his new backing singers, The Jordanaires. The sessions were nominally produced by Steve Sholes, the man who signed Presley to RCA, but for the

most part he very wisely let Elvis himself run the show. Like his best-selling debut, this album features a mixture of uptempo rockers, including no less than three Little Richard numbers, increasingly confident ballads like 'First In Line', and even a country weepie in 'Old Shep'.

Elvis went straight to Number One and stayed there for five weeks, earning him a second successive gold disc and once again proving that teenagers would buy rock 'n' roll albums as well as singles – but only if they were by Elvis Presley.

Number One singles:
None

Grammy awards: None

Label: US: RCA; UK: HMV

Recorded in: Hollywood, USA

Producer:
Steve Sholes

Personnel:
Elvis Presley (d. 1977)
Scotty Moore
Bill Black
D.J. Fontana
Dudley Brooks
The Jordanaires

1   **Rip It Up** (1:53)
2   **Love Me** (2:43)
3   **When My Blue Moon Turn To Gold Again** (2:21)
4   **Long Tall Sally** (1:53)
5   **First In Love** (3:34)
6   **Paralyzed** (2:23)
7   **So Glad You`re Mine** (2:20)
8   **Old Shep** (4:09)
9   **Ready Teddy** (1:56)
10 **Anyplace Is Paradise** (2:26)
11 **How`s The World Treating Me** (2:25)
12 **How Do You Think I Feel**   (2:12)

Total album length: 29 minutes

Elvis Presley

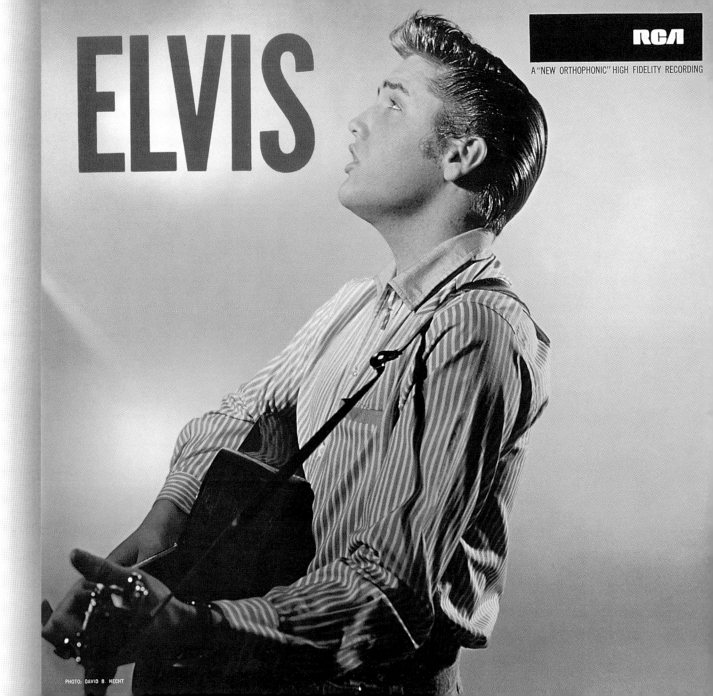

ELVIS

RCA

A "NEW ORTHOPHONIC" HIGH FIDELITY RECORDING

PHOTO: DAVID B. HECHT

25 | Frank Sinatra Sings For Only The Lonely

| • **Album sales:** 500,000 | • **Highest position:** 1 (5 weeks) | • **Release date:** 1958 |

During the late 1950s, when Frank Sinatra's career as an album-selling artist was at its peak, he liked to alternate between ballad-based albums and more upbeat collections. Thus, as Sinatra's first album for 1958 had been the exuberant *Come Fly With Me*, on *Sings For Only The Lonely* he took the tempo down again.

Sinatra had originally intended to record with Gordon Jenkins, who had worked as arranger on a number of his previous albums. However, Jenkins was unavailable at the time, so Sinatra hooked up once again with the arranger behind his first albums with Capitol, the widely-acclaimed Nelson Riddle. The result was what most critics agree to be one of the finest of Sinatra's ballad albums.

From the opening cut 'Only The Lonely' to the closing track 'One For My Baby', this set of songs follows a similar path to Sinatra's earlier down-tempo albums, except that this time he used a larger orchestra. The result was a sound on a grander scale, creating a dramatic, almost classical backdrop to the songs of love and loss.

The album struck a chord with the public. It spent five weeks at Number One and eventually became the only one of Sinatra's 1950s ballad albums to go gold.

Number One singles:
None

Grammy Awards:
Best album cover

Label: US: Capitol

Recorded: Hollywood, USA

Personnel:
Frank Sinatra (d 1998)
Nelson Riddle (d. 1985)

Producer:
Dave Cavanaugh

1 Only The Lonely (4:09)
2 Angel Eyes (3:44)
3 What's New? (5:12)
4 It's A Lonesome Old Town (4:16)
5 Willow Weep For Me (4:49)
6 Good-Bye (5:45)
7 Blues In The Night (4:45)
8 Guess I'll Hang My Tears Out To Dry (4:02)
9 Ebb Tide (3:17)
10 Spring Is Here (4:46)
11 Gone With The Wind (5:15)
12 One For My Baby (4:25)

Total album length: 54 minutes

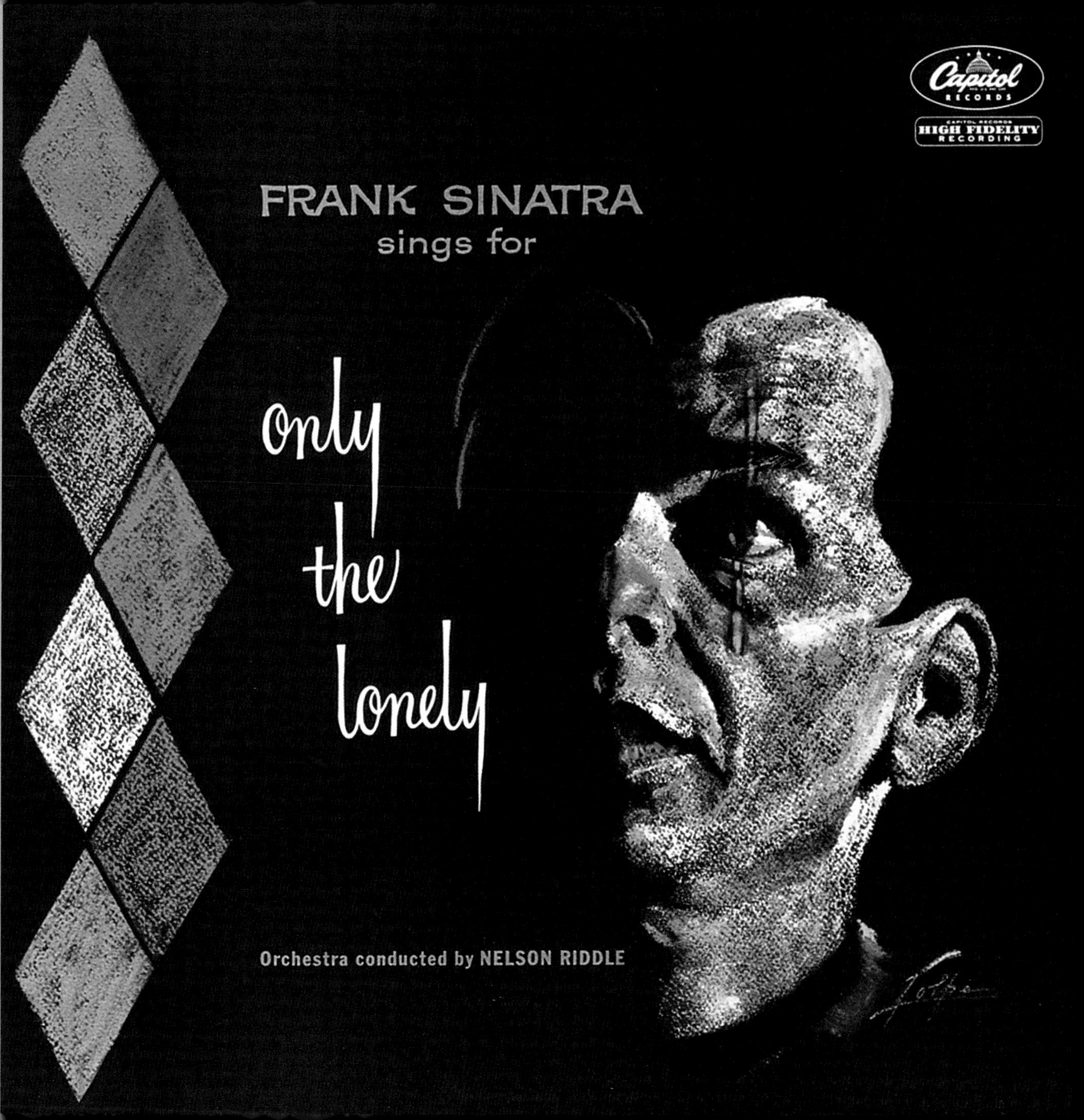

Capitol
RECORDS
HIGH FIDELITY
RECORDING
FRANK SINATRA
sings for
only the lonely
Orchestra conducted by NELSON RIDDLE

24 Belafonte

| • **Album sales:** 500,000 | • **Highest position:** 1 (6 weeks) | • **Release date:** 1956 |

Harry Belafonte's second album, released in 1956, featured numbers from the successful Broadway show *Three For Tonight,* which he had recently starred in. It also included material from his increasingly wide repertoire: many of the tracks were folk songs from the West Indies or traditional chain-gang songs from the plantations and prisons of the American south. The album established him as the one of the foremost black artists of the period, and remained at Number One on the Billboard charts for six weeks.

On the album, Belafonte revealed the full extent of his interpretive powers as a singer for the first time. The songs range from solemn Negro spirituals like 'Take My Mother Home', 'Noah', and 'In That Great Getting' Up Mornin' to lilting calypsos like 'Matilda'. 'Matilda' was one of Belafonte's most popular songs, and had been previously recorded as a single in 1953. This new recording was widely considered to be superior. Belafonte also tackled several black folk songs, including two from Leadbelly's repertoire ('Jump Down, Spin Around' and 'Sylvie').

Belafonte was backed on the album by an assortment of musicians, including guitarist Millard J Thomas, Tony Scott's Orchestra, and the Norman Luboff Choir.

Number One singles:
None

Grammy Awards:
None

Label: US: RCA Victor

Recorded in: New York & Hollywood, USA

Personnel:
Harry Belafonte
Millard J Thomas
Tony Scott and his
   Orchestra
The Norman Luboff
   Singers

Producer:
Henri René

1 **Waterboy (3:42)**
2 **Troubles (3:38)**
3 **Suzanne (3:19)**
4 **Matilda (3:34)**
5 **Take My Mother Home (6:00)**
6 **Noah (4:53)**
7 **Scarlet Ribbons (3:13)**
8 **In That Great Getting' Up Mornin' (3:15)**
9 **Unchained Melody (3:18)**
10 **Jump Down, Spin Around (1:54)**
11 **Sylvie (5:21)**

Total album length: 42 minutes

Harry Belafonte

LSP-1150 (e)

STEREO
Electronically Reprocessed

RCA VICTOR
A "New Orthophonic" High Fidelity Recording

WATERBOY
TROUBLES
SUZANNE
MATILDA
TAKE MY MOTHER HOME
NOAH
SCARLET RIBBONS
IN THAT GREAT GETTIN' UP MORNIN'
UNCHAINED MELODY
JUMP DOWN, SPIN AROUND
SYLVIE

Belafonte

© RCA Printed in U.S.A. RE

23 Sing Along With Mitch

| • **Album sales:** 500,000 | • **Highest position:** 1 (8 weeks) | • **Release date:** 1958 |

Mitch Miller was the most powerful figure in American popular music during the 1950s. He oversaw the output of Columbia Records, the era's most successful record label, and produced many of the label's key acts including Guy Mitchell and Johnny Mathis. However, for all his power and success few people imagined that the dapper middle-aged label boss would emerge as a star in his own right, let alone one of the best-selling artists of the decade.

The record that made his career was *Sing Along With Mitch*, a simple concept that became an enduring franchise on radio, TV and record over the next decade. The idea could hardly have been simpler – an all-male chorus sang simple versions of famous songs, from 'You Are My Sunshine' to 'She Wore A Yellow Ribbon', mostly

from the early part of the century, and the American public was urged to sing along, helped out by the inclusion of lyric sheets.

To the amazement of the music industry, *Sing Along With Mitch* went to the top of the charts and remained at Number One for eight weeks, knocking Elvis' *King Creole* off the top spot, and earning a gold record along the way.

Number One singles:
None

Grammy awards:
None

Recorded in: New York, USA

Label: US: Columbia

Personnel:
Mitch Miller And The Gang

Producer:
Mitch Miller

1   **That Old Gang Of Mine** (2:06)
2   **Down By The Old Mill Stream** (2:37)
3   **By The Light Of The Silvery Moon** (2:15)
4   **You Are My Sunshine** (3:18)
5   **Till We Meet Again** (2:44)
6   **Sweet Violets** (2:42)
7   **Let The Rest Of The World Go By** (3:04)
8   **I've Got Sixpence/I've Been Working On The Railroad/That's Where My Money Goes** (4:03)
9   **She Wore A Yellow Ribbon** (2:49)
10 **Don't Fence Me In** (2:05)
11 **There Is A Tavern In The Town/Show Me The Way To Go Home** (3:23)
12 **Bell Bottom Trousers/Be Kind To Your Web-Footed Friends** (2:54)

Total album length: 34 minutes

CS 8004

 **STEREO** COLUMBIA GUARANTEED HIGH FIDELITY

SING ALONG WITH MITCH
MITCH MILLER & THE GANG

THAT OLD GANG OF MINE DOWN BY THE OLD MILL STREAM

BY THE LIGHT OF THE SILVERY MOON YOU ARE MY SUNSHINE

(SMILE AWHILE) TILL WE MEET AGAIN SWEET VIOLETS

LET THE REST OF THE WORLD GO BY MEDLEY: I'VE GOT SIXPENCE;

I'VE BEEN WORKING ON THE RAILROAD; THAT'S WHERE MY MONEY GOES

SHE WORE A YELLOW RIBBON DON'T FENCE ME IN

THERE IS A TAVERN IN THE TOWN & SHOW ME THE WAY TO GO HOME

BELL BOTTOM TROUSERS & BE KIND TO YOUR WEB-FOOTED FRIENDS

22 Here We Go Again!

| • **Album sales:** 500,000 | • **Highest position:** 1 (8 weeks) | • **Release date:** October 1959 |

By the time they recorded *Here We Go Again!*, in the summer of 1959, The Kingston Trio were firmly established as the most popular group in America – not just the most popular folk group but the most popular group of any kind. Not until the arrival of The Beatles would anyone dominate the album charts to such an extent. Following the album's release, in October 1959, The Kingston Trio had no less than four albums in the Top 10 simultaneously.

As its title suggests, *Here We Go Again!* saw the Trio sticking faithfully to the formula that had already brought them so much success. The only change was that the songs were a little less widely assorted in their origins. Most of them were American and they were all in English, apart from 'E Inu Tatou E', a song from Guard and Shane's native Hawaii. Standouts included the Top-20 single 'Worried Man' (adapted from the Carter Family's 'Worried Man Blues') and the dramatic ballad 'San Miguel'.

Here We Go Again! went rapidly up to Number One in the charts, where it remained for eight weeks, during an overall chart stay of 40 weeks, earning the Trio yet another gold record.

Number One singles:
None

Grammy awards:
None

Label: US: Capitol

Recorded in: Hollywood, USA

Personnel:
Bob Shane
Nick Reynolds
Dave Guard

Producer:
Voyle Gilmore

1   Molly Dee (1:45)
2   Across The Wide Missouri (3:02)
3   Haul Away (2:25)
4   Wanderer (2:29)
5   'Round About the Mountain (2:41)
6   Oleanna (1:56)
7   Unfortunate Miss Bailey (2:17)
8   San Miguel (2:15)
9   E Inu Tatou E (1:52)
10 Rollin' Stone (2:35)
11 Goober Peas (2:20)
12 Worried Man (2:53)

Total album length: 28 minutes

21 Elvis Presley

| • **Album sales:** 500,000 | • **Highest position:** 1 (10 weeks) | • **Release date:** March 1956 |

Elvis Presley's self-titled debut album was a truly revolutionary record, an undisputed rock'n'roll classic. At the time it was also a very risky one. RCA had just signed Elvis from Sun Records on the basis of a handful of singles. At the time the received wisdom was that rock'n'roll was exclusively suited to singles. But when Presley's debut single for the label, 'Heartbreak Hotel', hit the top of the charts, RCA decided to take a chance and follow it up with an album.

The album in question was primarily recorded in two sessions at RCA's studios in Nashville, then filled out with five tracks Elvis had recorded 18 months earlier at Sun Studios. The band was Elvis' classic backing trio – Scotty Moore, Bill Black and DJ Fontana – plus a little piano and some backing vocals. The material was the music Elvis loved: rock'n'roll, blues and country. It included a hit single in 'Blue Suede Shoes', and a signature ballad performance in his reworking of Rodgers and Hart's 'Blue Moon'.

RCA's gamble paid off handsomely. *Elvis Presley* was the first rock'n'roll album to reach the Number One slot. It remained there for 10 weeks, going gold in the process.

Number One singles:
None

Grammy awards: None

Label: US: RCA Victor;
UK: HMV

Recorded in: Nashville &
Memphis, USA

Personnel:
Elvis Presley (d. 1977)
Scotty Moore
Bill Black
D.J. Fontana
Chet Atkins
Floyd Cramer
Gordon Stroker
Ben & Brock Speer

Producer:
Steve Sholes

1 Blue Suede Shoes (2:00)
2 I`m Counting On You (2:25)
3 I Got A Woman (2:25)
4 One Sided Love Affair (2:11)
5 I Love You Because (2:44)
6 Just Because (2:34)
7 Tutti Frutti (1:59)
8 Tryin` To Get To You (2:32)
9 I`m Gonna Sit Right Down And Cry (Over You) (2:03)
10 I`ll Never Let You Go (2:26)
11 Blue Moon (2:41)
12 Money Honey (2:36)

Total album length: 29 minutes

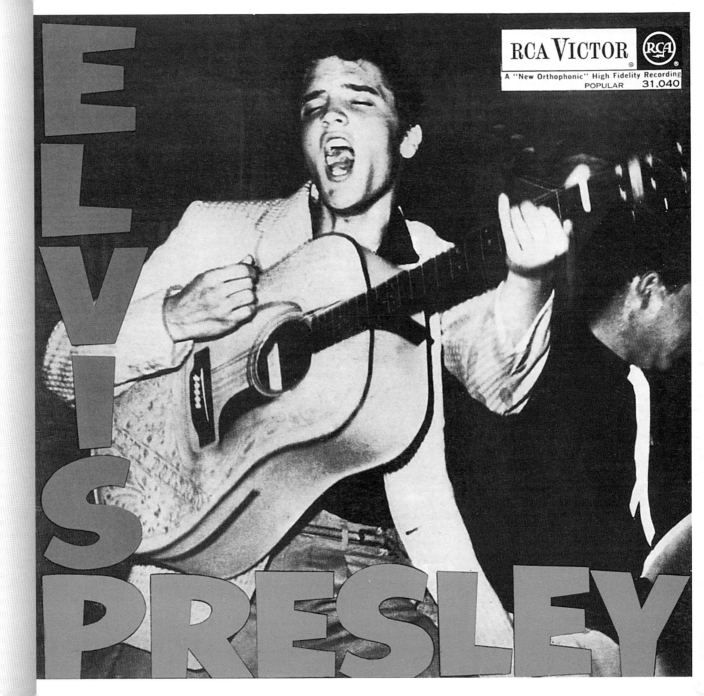

20 Loving You

• **Album sales:** 500,000 | • **Highest position:** 1 (10 weeks) | • **Release date:** July 1957 |

Elvis' third album, *Loving You*, was released just as it was becoming clear that Elvis was a bigger star than pop music had ever previously produced. His popularity just seemed to keep on growing. He had Number One single after Number One single and he'd appeared in two movies, the second of which was *Loving You*.

Despite appearances, this is not strictly a soundtrack album. It includes all seven songs that Elvis sings in the movie, but the remaining five songs are new recordings. Neither are the movie songs recorded with studio orchestras; the whole album was performed by Elvis' regular band and recorded in his regular studio.

Overall, *Loving You* is not such a hard-rocking set as his two previous albums. The title track in particular reveals the new influence of crooners like Dean Martin. However, there is still plenty of classic rock'n'roll here, including the opening 'Mean Woman Blues' and the hit single 'Teddy Bear', as well as straight-ahead country and blues in 'Have I Told You Lately (That I Love You)' and 'I Need You So'.

Loving You took just two weeks to make it to the Number One slot and remained there for 10 weeks, going gold in the process.

Number One singles:
US: Teddy Bear

Grammy awards:
None

Label: US & UK: RCA

Recorded in: Hollywood, USA

Personnel:
Elvis Presley (d. 1977)
Scotty Moore
Bill Black
D.J. Fontana
Dudley Brooks
The Jordanaires

Producer:
Steve Sholes

1   Mean Woman Blues (2:18)
2   (Let Me Be Your) Teddy Bear (1:52)
3   Loving You (2:18)
4   Got A Lot O' Livin' To Do (2:34)
5   Lonesome Cowboy (3:07)
6   Hot Dog (1:17)
7   Party (1:31)
8   Blueberry Hill (2:40)
9   True Love (2:07)
10 Don't Leave Me Now (2:06)
11 Have I Told You Lately (That I Love You) (2:33)
12 I Need You So (2:37)

Total album length: 27 minutes

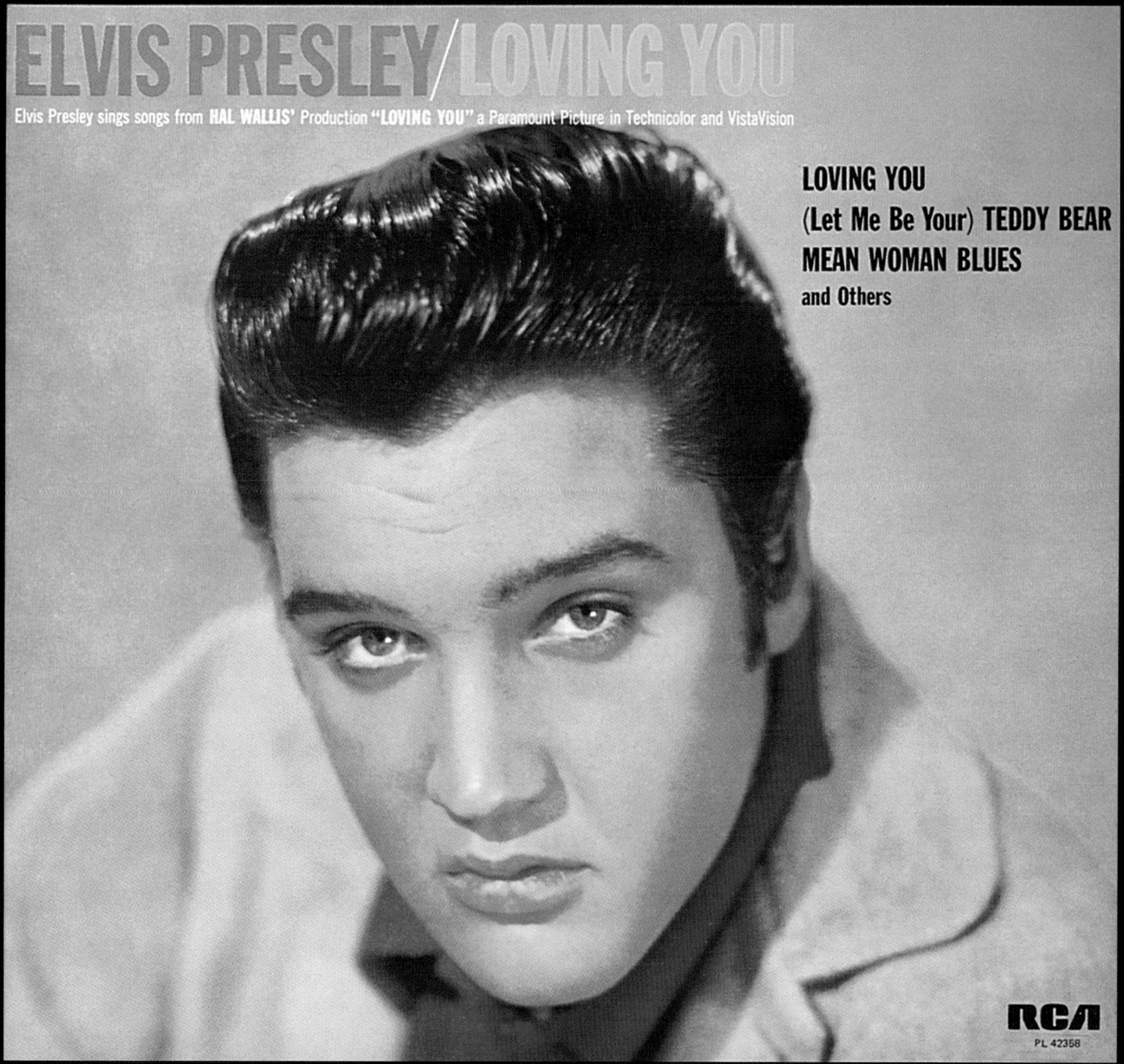

ELVIS PRESLEY/LOVING YOU

Elvis Presley sings songs from **HAL WALLIS'** Production **"LOVING YOU"** a Paramount Picture in Technicolor and VistaVision

LOVING YOU
(Let Me Be Your) TEDDY BEAR
MEAN WOMAN BLUES
and Others

Sleeve artwork by Bud Fraker

RCA
PL 42358

19 The Music From Peter Gunn

| • **Album sales:** 500,000 | • **Highest position:** 1 (10 weeks) | • **Release date:** 1959 |

Henry Mancini was just about to be fired from his staff job as a composer for Universal Pictures when he was offered the chance to score a new TV detective show, *Peter Gunn*, for which the director, Blake Edwards, wanted a jazz feel. Mancini was well qualified for this, having written recently the jazz-inflected score for Orson Welles' *Touch Of Evil*. For *Peter Gunn* he used an 11-piece jazz ensemble featuring sax legend Plas Johnson along with Shelly Manne on drums, Victor Feldman on vibes, and the future film composer John Williams on piano. Stylistically Mancini borrowed heavily from cool jazz, a sound previously unknown to most television viewers.

The TV series became the surprise hit of the new season, helped in no small part by the music, in particular the pounding theme tune. In response to the show's popularity, RCA decided to release an album featuring the soundtrack. The result exceeded all expectations. It leapt up to Number One in the charts and remained there for 10 weeks. In all it spent more than two years on the charts and won two Grammy awards. It also prompted many Americans to buy new stereo hi-fis in order to appreciate it properly.

Number One singles:
None

Grammy awards:
Album of the year; Best arrangement

Label: US: RCA Victor

Recorded in: Hollywood, USA

Producer:
Simon Rady

Personnel:
Henry Mancini (d. 1994)
Plas Johnson
Shelley Manne
John Williams
Victor Feldman
Jack Sperling
Rolly Bundock
Pete Candoli
Ted Nash
Dick Nash
Milt Bernhart
Ronnie Lang
Larry Bunker
Johnny T Williams

1 Peter Gunn (2:07)
2 Sorta Blue (2:58)
3 The Brothers Go To Mother's (2:57)
4 Dreamsville (3:56)
5 Session At Pete's Pad (4:00)
6 Soft Sounds (3:35)
7 Fallout! (3:16)
8 The Floater (3:18)
9 Slow And Easy (3:07)
10 A Profound Gass (3:20)
11 Brief And Breezy (3:33)
12 Not From Dixie (4:10)

Total album length: 40 minutes

Henry Mancini

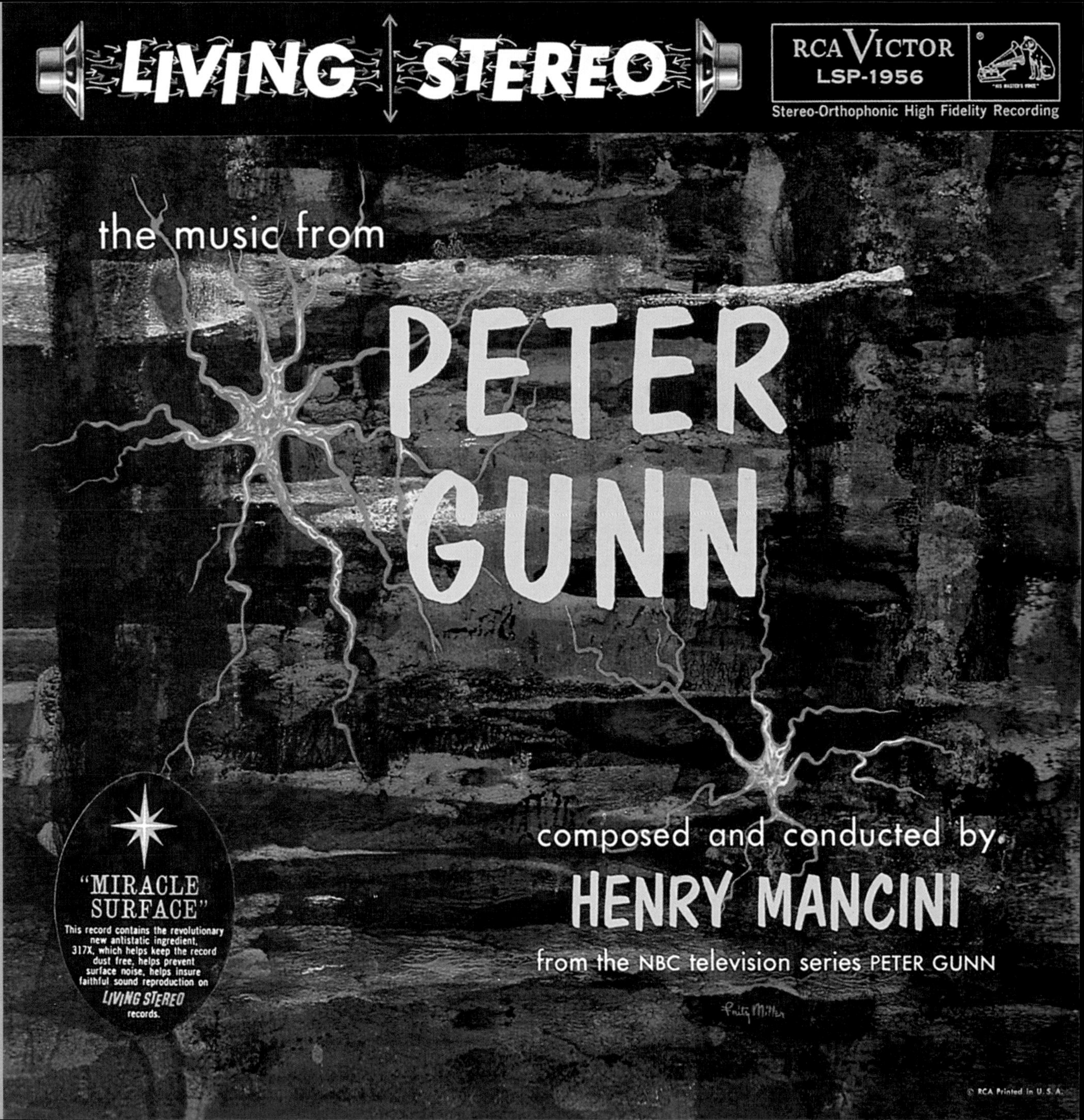

◄◄ LIVING ‡ STEREO ►►

RCA VICTOR
LSP-1956
Stereo-Orthophonic High Fidelity Recording

the music from

PETER
GUNN

composed and conducted by

HENRY MANCINI

from the NBC television series PETER GUNN

"MIRACLE
SURFACE"
This record contains the revolutionary
new antistatic ingredient,
317X, which helps keep the record
dust free, helps prevent
surface noise, helps insure
faithful sound reproduction on
LIVING STEREO
records.

Fritz Miller

© RCA Printed in U.S.A.

18 At Large

• **Album sales:** 500,000 │ • **Highest position:** 1 (15 weeks) │ • **Release date:** June 1959 │

*A*t Large was The Kingston Trio's first album to be recorded after their lightning rise to fame as a result of the success of *Tom Dooley*. Their previous albums had been quickly recorded affairs – they were essentially just studio versions of their live show – but this time the trio used their new-found status to take full advantage of the possibilities of studio recording.

At Large was recorded in stereo, which was a new development at the time. With the aid of Sinatra's producer Voyle Gilmore, the Trio experimented with multi-tracking overdubs of both vocals and instruments. The result. unsurprisingly. was a far more sophisticated affair than their previous albums. *At Large* is a varied collection which includes plenty of upbeat

material, like the sea shanty 'Blow Ye Winds' and the Calypso-styled Bob Shane original 'I Bawled', alongside delicate numbers like 'All My Sorrows' and 'The Seine'.

At Large also yielded two hit singles for the group: 'Scarlet Ribbons' and the gentle protest song 'MTA'. The success of these singles helped propel the album all the way to the Number One spot, where it remained for an extraordinary 15 weeks on the way to becoming the Trio's third successive gold album.

Number One singles:
None

Grammy Awards:
Best performance – folk

Label: US & UK: Capitol

Recorded in: Hollywood, USA

Personnel:
Bob Shane
Nick Reynolds
Dave Guard

Producer:
Voyle Gilmore

1   MTA (3:14)
2   All My Sorrows (2:48)
3   Blow Ye Winds (2:00)
4   Corey, Corey (2:06)
5   The Seine (2:40)
6   I Bawled (1:52)
7   Good News (2:01)
8   Getaway John (2:36)
9   Long Black Rifle (3:04)
10 Early In The Mornin' (2:04)
11 Scarlet Ribbons (2:17)
12 Remember The Alamo (2:59)

Total album length: 30 minutes

THE KINGSTON TRIO AT LARGE

The Sound Of Music

| • **Album sales:** 500,000 | • **Highest position:** 1 (16 weeks) | • **Release date:** November 1959 |

The Sound Of Music – which most people will identify with the 1965 Robert Wise film, one of the most popular movie musicals of all time – was the biggest success in the illustrious career of composers Rodgers and Hammerstein. The story is based on that of Maria von Trapp, a young Viennese woman who is educated in a convent and goes on to become a governess. She falls in love with her employer and the family take to the stage as a troupe of singers. This emotional story of romantic passion is set against a backdrop of the rise of fascism.

The original soundtrack of the Broadway show was a milestone in the career of Mary Martin, who played the role of Maria. Despite her elderly-sounding voice (she was aged 40 at the time of the Broadway premiere) she sings with warmth and charisma. Rodgers and Hammerstein, who also acted as co-producers, wrote some of their best-known numbers for the show. Ranging from the winsome 'My Favorite Things', 'Do-Re-Mi' and 'Sixteen Going On Seventeen' to the anthemic 'Climb Ev'ry Mountain'.

The Sound of Music ran on Broadway for 1443 performances, and this recorded version became a bestselling LP.

1   **Praludium: The Sound Of Music (5:08)**
2   **Maria (3:21)**
3   **My Favorite Things (2:47)**
4   **Do-Re-Mi (5:53)**
5   **Sixteen Going On Seventeen (3:50)**
6   **The Lonely Goatherd (3:21)**
7   **How Can Love Survive? (3:03)**
8   **The Sound Of Music (3:14)**
9   **Laendler (2:24)**
10 **So Long, Farewell (2:51)**
11 **Climb Ev'ry Mountain (3:31)**
12 **No Way To Stop It (3:05)**
13 **An Ordinary Couple (3:36)**
14 **Processional (3:48)**
15 **Sixteen Going On Seventeen (reprise) (2:16)**
16 **Edelweiss (2:06)**
17 **Climb Ev'ry Mountain (reprise) (1:36)**

Total album length: 56 minutes

Number One singles:
None

Grammy awards:
None

Label: US: Columbia; UK: Philips

Recorded in: N/A

Personnel:
Mary Martin (d. 1990)
Theodore Bikel

Producer:
Godard Lieberson
Richard Rogers
Oscar Hammerstein II

The Sound of Music

ORIGINAL BROADWAY CAST

This Columbia High Fidelity recording is scientifically designed to play with the highest quality of reproduction on the phonograph of your choice, new or old. If you are the owner of a new stereophonic system, this record will play with even more brilliant true-to-life fidelity. In short, you can purchase this record with no fear of its becoming obsolete in the future.

16 Calypso

| • **Album sales:** 500,000 | • **Highest position:** 1 (31 weeks) | • **Release date:** June 1956 |

Released in 1956, *Calypso* established Harry Belafonte as a major star and had a huge influence on American folk music. Until its release, Belafonte had recorded in a number of folk styles, but this set of songs were all West Indian calypsos, ranging from the romantic to the humorous. Songwriter Irving Burgie, otherwise known as Lord Burgess, wrote the majority of the songs on the album, some in conjunction with William Attaway, another black songwriter, and Harry Belafonte himself.

Two of the album tracks, 'The Banana Boat Song (Day-O)' and 'Jamaica Farewell', became big hit singles for Belafonte, while others, such as the romantic 'I Do Adore Her' and 'Come Back Liza', remained part of his repertoire for years to come. Providing contrast to the love ballads are the comic songs like 'The Jack-Ass Song', 'Will His Love Be Like His Rum?', and 'Man Smart (Woman Smarter)', which introduced the witty and mischievous aspect of calypso to the album's white audience.

On its release, the album went straight to the top of the charts and remained there for 31 weeks. In total, the album spent an extraordinary 99 weeks on the charts, becoming one of the era's top-selling albums by a solo artist.

Number One singles:
None

Grammy awards: None

Label: US: RCA Victor;
UK: HMV

Recorded in: Hollywood,
USA

Personnel:
Harry Belafonte
Tony Scott
Millard J. Thomas

Producers:
Henri René
Joe Reisman
E.O. Welker
Herman Diaz Jnr

1 Banana Boat Song (Day-O) (3:02)
2 I Do Adore Her (2:48)
3 Jamaica Farewell (3:02)
4 Will His Love Be Like His Rum? (2:33)
5 Dolly Dawn (3:13)
6 Star-O (2:02)
7 The Jack-Ass Song (2:52)
8 Hosanna (2:34)
9 Come Back Liza (3:03)
10 Brown Skin Girl (2:43)
11 Man Smart (Woman Smarter) (3:31)

Total album length: 31 minutes

RCA VICTOR
LPM-1248
A "NEW ORTHOPHONIC" HIGH FIDELITY RECORDING

HARRY BELAFONTE CALYPSO

PHOTO. ROY STEVENS

© RCA Printed in U.S.A.

15 South Pacific

| • **Album sales:** 500,000 | • **Highest position:** 1 (31 weeks) | • **Release date:** March 1958 |

The *South Pacific* film soundtrack was the bestselling album of 1958, the year of its release. The film bore a very close resemblance to the stage show, mainly because its composers, Richard Rodgers and Oscar Hammerstein, had maintained a great deal of control in its production. The film soundtrack included all the songs from the original Broadway show, plus 'My Girl Back Home', which had previously been cut.

The story of *South Pacific* dealt with the complications of two inter-racial love affairs, one between a young nurse and an older man with two half-Polynesian children, the other between an American serviceman and a beautiful island girl. The tense racial and sexual themes were explored in songs ranging from the exotic 'Bali H'ai' to the comic 'I'm Gonna Wash That Man Right Outa My Hair'. Mitzi Gaynor starred on screen as female lead Nellie Forbush and sang her own songs, including the hit 'I'm In Love With A Wonderful Guy', while other characters in the on-screen cast had their voices dubbed on by other singers: the opera singer Giorgio Tozzi took the role of Emile DeBecque, played on screen by Rossanno Brazzi, for the showstopping 'Some Enchanted Evening'.

Number One singles:
None

Grammy awards:
None

Label: US & UK: RCA

Recorded in: N/A

Producer: N/A

Personnel:
Mitzi Gaynor
Giorgio Tozzi
Ray Walston
Bill Lee
Muriel Smith
Thurl Ravenscroft
Joshua Logan
Ken Darby
Ed Powell
Alfred Newman
Ken Darby Singers

1 **South Pacific Overture** (3:03)
2 **Dites-Moi** (1:19)
3 **A Cockeyed Optimist** (1:45)
4 **Twin Soliloquies/Some Enchanted Evening** (5:53)
5 **Bloody Mary** (1:57)
6 **My Girl Back Home** (1:42)
7 **There Is Nothin' Like A Dame** (3:50)
8 **Bali Ha'I** (3:41)
9 **I'm Gonna Wash That Man Right Outa My Hair** (2:56)
10 **I'm In Love with A Wonderful Guy** (3:23)
11 **Younger Than Springtime** (4:59)
12 **Happy Talk** (3:46)
13 **Honey Bun** (1:48)
14 **Carefully Taught** (1:15)
15 **This Nearly Was Mine** (2:12)
16 **Finale** (2:58)

Total album length: 46 minutes

14 The Unforgettable Nat King Cole

| • **Album sales:** 1,000,000 | • **Highest position:** 30 | • **Release date:** 1952 |

The year 1952, when the *The Unforgettable* album was released, saw Nat King Cole at the height of his success. The previous year he had dissolved his group, the Nat King Cole Trio, and established himself as a solo artist, scoring his fourth Number One hit and gold record with 'Too Young', which topped the charts in June 1951. The follow-up single 'Unforgettable' didn't fare quite as well at the time of release, peaking at Number 14, although it has since become one of his most celebrated recordings.

Up to this point, Cole's pop success had been mainly with singles releases, while his albums had on the whole been jazzier affairs. Now he decided the time was right for a pop album release so he compiled the two hits, together with other recent single releases like the chart-topping 'Mona Lisa', to make what was initially a 10-inch album. The album, also entitled *Unforgettable*, was reissued as a 12-inch LP in 1954 and once again in March 1965.

Released before *Billboard* magizine began their album chart, *Unforgettable* didn't appear on the charts until 1965, when it was re-released following Cole's untimely death. It had by then sold over a million copies.

Number One singles:
US: Mona Lisa; Too Young

Grammy awards:
None

Label: US: Capitol

Recorded in: N/A

Personnel:
Nat King Cole (d. 1965)

Producer: N/A

1   Unforgettable (3:13)
2   Portrait of Jennie (3:09)
3   What'll I Do? (3:05)
4   Lost April (2:58)
5   Answer Me, My Love (2:07)
6   Hajji Baba (3:07)
7   Too Young (3:13)
8   Mona Lisa (3:16)
9   (I Love You) For Sentimental Reasons (2:54)
10 Red Sails In The Sunset (3:17)
11 Pretend (2:44)
12 Make Her Mine (2:57)

Total album length: 36 minutes

Nat King Cole

THE
UNFORGETTABLE
NAT KING COLE

WITH COMMENTARY BY ALAN DELL

13 A Jolly Christmas From Frank Sinatra

| • **Album sales:** 1,000,000 | • **Highest position:** 18 | • **Release date:** November 1957 |

In Christmas 1957, Frank Sinatra's recording career was at a high. Over the previous year he had had hits with albums as diverse as the string quartet-backed *Close To You* and the upbeat *A Swingin' Affair*. Most recently he'd charted with the soundtrack to his latest movie, *Pal Joey*.

One thing that Sinatra had not released, thus far, was a Christmas album. Sinatra went into the studio with arranger Gordon Jenkins and set to work fashioning an album that blended the religious, such as 'Silent Night' or 'O Little Town Of Bethlehem', with cheerily secular seasonal standards such as 'Jingle Bells'. Jenkins' arrangements, full of strings and vocal choruses were considered by some critics at the time to be in poor taste. The record label, Capitol,

decided to round the album out by including two tracks ('White Christmas' and 'Christmas Waltz') that Sinatra had previously recorded with his long-term arranger Nelson Riddle, back in 1954.

The public did not immediately take to the album. On release it only made Number 18 in the charts, but Sinatra's lasting popularity meant that it has become a Christmas perennial. To date, it has sold over a million copies.

Number One singles:
None

Grammy awards:
None

Label: US & UK: Capitol

Recorded in: Hollywood, USA

Personnel:
Frank Sinatra (d. 1998)
The Ralph Brewster Singers
Gordon Jenkins
Nelson Riddle (d. 1985)

Producer:
Voyle Gilmore

1   Jingle Bells (2:00)
2   Christmas Song (3:28)
3   Mistletoe And Holly (2:18)
4   I'll Be Home For Christmas (3:11)
5   Christmas Waltz (3:03)
6   Have Yourself A Merry Little Christmas (3:29)
7   First Noel (2:44)
8   Hark! The Herald Angels Sing (2:24)
9   O Little Town Of Bethlehem (2:06)
10 Adeste Fideles (2:34)
11 It Came upon A Midnight Clear (2:51)
12 Silent Night (2:31)
13 White Christmas (2:37)

Total album length: 35 minutes

Frank Sinatra

a Jolly Christmas from frank Sinatra

with the orchestra and chorus of GORDON JENKINS

12 The Star Carol

| • Album sales: 1,000,000 | • Highest position: 4 | • Release date: October 1958 |

Tennessee Ernie Ford's first album of devotional songs, *Hymns*, had been the biggest selling album of his career to date – it remained on Billboard's Top Album charts for a remarkable 277 consecutive weeks. So, given the general popularity of Christmas albums in the 1950s, it was hardly a surprise that come Christmas time 1958, Ford should decide to follow up with an album of Christmas carols.

At this time Ford was firmly based in Los Angeles, where he recorded his weekly Thursday night NBC variety show, simply called *The Ford Show*. The show topped the ratings and was one of the most popular TV shows of the era. To record *The Star Carol*, Ford went into Capitol Records' Hollywood recording studio,

accompanied by his long-time arranger Jack Fascinato, and set to work. The songs they chose were Christmas favourites, from 'O Little Town Of Bethlehem' to the inevitable closer, 'Silent Night', all sung in Ford's trademark voice: a rich, booming baritone.

The public responded with great enthusiasm, and *The Star Carol* soon matched the achievement of *Hymns* in selling over a million copies. It was one of only a handful of albums from the 1950s to achieve such a feat. So popular was it that it returned to the charts the following two Christmases.

Number One singles:
None

Grammy awards: None

Label: US & UK: Capitol

Recorded in: Hollywood, USA

Personnel:
Tennessee Ernie Ford
(d. 1991)
Jack Fascinato

Producer:
Lee Gillette

1   Joy To The World
2   O Little Town Of Bethlehem
3   The Star Carol
4   Hark, The Herald Angels Sing
5   Some Children See Him
6   God Rest Ye Merry Gentlemen
7   O Harken Ye
8   Adeste Fideles
9   The First Noel
10 We Three Kings
11 It Came Upon A Midnight Clear
12 Silent Night

Official track times not available

T h e STAR CAROL

"Tennessee" Ernie Ford
SINGS HIS CHRISTMAS FAVORITES

11 Hymns

| • **Album sales:** 1,000,000 | • **Highest position:** 2 | • **Release date:** 1957 |

In the spring of 1957, Tennessee Ernie Ford was in the midst of transforming himself from a country and western singer (best known for his chart-topping single '16 Tons') into an all-round entertainer and TV presenter, known for his catchphrase 'Bless your little pea-pickin' hearts'. His TV show, *The Ford Show*, had debuted on NBC in the fall of 1956, and by the end of its first season was Number One in the ratings.

Ford had fought with TV executives to be allowed to finish each show with a spiritual number. To the producers' surprise, this turned out to be one of the most successful sections of the show. In response to huge popular demand, Ford decided to make his next album exclusively devotional in nature. Simply entitled *Hymns*, the album combined famous numbers like 'Rock Of Ages' and 'The Old Rugged Cross' along with lesser-known selections such as 'In The Garden'. The material was ideally suited to Ford's powerful voice and it quickly became the biggest hit album of his career.

Hymns was the first religious album to go gold. It remained on the charts for an unprecedented 277 weeks, breaking all records and eventually selling over a million copies. In 1963, *Hymns* was honoured by Capitol as being the most successful LP ever recorded by a Capitol artist. His subsequent album *Great Gospel Songs* won a Grammy award in 1964.

Number One singles:
None

Grammy awards:
None

Recorded in:
Los Angeles, USA

Label: US: Capitol

Personnel:
Tennessee Ernie Ford
(d. 1991)
Jack Fascinato

Producer: N/A

1   Who At My Door Is Standing (3:18)
2   Rock Of Ages (2:28)
3   Softly And Tenderly (2:43)
4   Sweet Hour Of Prayer (2:51)
5   My Task (2:15)
6   Let The Lower Lights Be Burning (2:02)
7   The Ninety And Nine (2:35)
8   The Old Rugged Cross (2:41)
9   When They Ring Those Golden Bells (3:34)
10 In The Garden (2:45)
11 Ivory Palaces (3:01)
12 Others (2:41)

Total album length: 33 minutes

Tennessee Ernie Ford:
Hymns

10 Time Out

| • **Album sales:** 1,000,000 | • **Highest position:** 2 | • **Release date:** June 1959 |

Dave Brubeck was already a major star on the jazz circuit when he came to record *Time Out* in the summer of 1959. His quartet, featuring the great alto player and composer Paul Desmond, seemed to personify the classically influenced, cool jazz style of the late 1950s. *Time Out*, however, was conceived as an experimental work. The title referred to Brubeck's decision to make a record which would stray outside the conventional 3/4 and 4/4 time signatures.

The record company were not enthusiastic at first, but Brubeck had an ace up his sleeve. Paul Desmond had written a tune in 5/4 time, simply called 'Take Five', that was so instantly memorable that all objections were swept away. 'Take Five' was so addictively catchy that it

became that rare thing, a million-selling jazz hit single. There were also other popular tracks on the album, which critics now consider to be a perfect balance between the experimental and the accessible. These include the Turkish-influenced 'Blue Rondo A La Turk' and the delicately arranged 'Strange Meadow Lark'.

Time Out's slow-building popularity saw it climb to Number Two on the album charts and eventually go on to sell over a million copies.The distinctive, jazz-inspired painting on album cover is by Neil Fujita, Director of Design and Packaging at Columbia Records from 1954–60.

The Dave Brubeck Quartet

Number One singles:
None

Grammy awards:
None

Label: US & UK: Columbia

Recorded in: New York, USA

Personnel:
Dave Brubeck
Paul Desmond
Eugene Wright
Joe Morello

Producer:
Teo Macero

1 **Blue Rondo A La Turk** (6:44)
2 **Strange Meadow Lark** (7:22)
3 **Take Five** (5:24)
4 **Three To Get Ready** (5:24)
5 **Kathy's Waltz** (4:48)
6 **Everybody's Jumpin'** (4:23)
7 **Pick Up Sticks** (4:16)

Total album length: 40 minutes

TIME OUT
THE DAVE BRUBECK QUARTET

BLUE RONDO A LA TURK • STRANGE MEADOW LARK • TAKE FIVE • THREE TO GET READY • KATHY'S WALTZ • EVERYBODY'S JUMPIN' • PICK UP STICKS

Sleeve artwork by Neil Fujits

fontana

The Music Man

9

| • **Album sales:** 1,000,000 | • **Highest position:** 1 | • **Release date:** January 1958 |

The Music Man opened at the Majestic Theatre, New York in December 1957 and ran 1,379 performances, establishing its composer Meredith Willson as one of the leading figures of American musical theatre. The cast recording of the show became one of the biggest-selling albums of the decade, and several of the songs, including 'Seventy-Six Trombones' and 'Till There was You' became all-time classics.

The story of *The Music Man* told of a small Iowa community who club together to create a marching band for their children. The characters and setting were drawn from Willson's own Midwestern boyhood and events take place in around 1912. The part of Harold Hill, a con man who arrives in town and is converted into a decent, law-abiding citizen, was memorably played by Robert Preston, whose songs feature rapid-fire, percussive effects. The more romantic songs were sung by Barbara Cook, who played Marian, the librarian that Hill falls in love with.

Cook's singing became one of the highlights of the album. The duet 'Till There Was You' lived on, notably with The Beatles' cover version on their 1963 album *With the Beatles*.

Number One singles:
None

Grammy Awards: Best original cast album (Broadway or TV)

Label: US & UK: Capitol

Recorded in: New York, USA

Personnel:
Barbara Cook
Robert Preston
Eddie Hodges
Pert Kelton
Herbert Greene
Dick Jones
Verne Reed
Paul Reed
Buffalo Bills
Adnia Rice
Peggy Mondo
Elaine Swann
Adam Hodges
Iggie Wolfington Ensemble
Bob Norbert Orchestra

Producer: N/A

1 Overture/Rock Island (5:29)
2 Iowa Stubborn (1:59)
3 Ya Got Trouble (3:48)
4 Piano Lesson (1:56)
5 Good Night My Someone (2:46)
6 Seventy-six Trombones (3:01)
7 Sincere (1:40)
8 The Sadder-But-Wiser Girl For Me (1:41)
9 Pick-A-Little, Take-A-Little/Goodnight (1:57)
10 Goodnight Ladies/Marian the Librarian (2:44)
11 My White Knight (3:02)
12 Wells Fargo Wagon (2:13)
13 It's You (1:25)
14 Shipoopi (2:11)
15 Lida Rose/Will I Ever Tell You? (4:17)
16 Gary, Indiana (1:25)
17 Till There Was You (2:46)

Total album length: 44 minutes

Original Cast Recording

Love Is The Thing

| • **Album sales:** 1,000,000 | • **Highest position:** 1 | • **Release date:** 1957 |

Nat 'King' Cole's *Love Is The Thing* proved a million seller for Capitol Records on its release in 1957. Among its many hit songs was 'Stardust', which had been issued on EP earlier in the year. Composer Hoagy Carmichael said it was his favourite version of the song, reviving as it did the original introduction to the verse, and it became one of America's best-loved songs.

Throughout the album, arranger Gordon Jenkins provided a lush orchestral backdrop to Cole's understated yet carefully enunciated vocals. The result was to create a romantic mood that rendered Cole's limited vocal range irrelevant. As Cole himself put it: 'I lean heavily on the lyrics. I try to tell a story with the melody as background'. The combination of Jenkins' swooning strings and Cole's relaxed, urbane singing style gave a classic feel to every track on the album, including the most sentimental ballads and the most hackneyed jazz standards.

The success of *Love Is The Thing* helped to establish Cole not just as a 'sepia Sinatra' but also as the leading ballad singer of his time during a period when race was still considered by record companies to be a major obstacle to mainstream sales potential.

Number One singles:
None

Grammy awards:
None

Label: US & UK: Capitol

Recorded in: N/A

Personnel:
Nat 'King' Cole (d. 1965)
Gordon Jenkins and his orchestra

Producer: N/A

1 **When I Fall In love** (3:11)
2 **End Of A Love Affair** (3:22)
3 **Stardust** (3:15)
4 **Stay As Sweet As You Are** (2:59)
5 **Where Can I Go Without You** (2:57)
6 **Maybe It's Because I Love You Too Much** (2:50)
7 **Love Letters** (2:46)
8 **Ain't Misbehavin'** (3:17)
9 **I Thought About Marie** (3:06)
10 **At Last** (3:00)
11 **It's All In The Game** (3:07)
12 **When Sunny Gets Blue** (2:46)
13 **Love Is The Thing** (3:01)

Total album length: 40 minutes

Love is the Thing

the voice of
NAT "KING" COLE

with the orchestra of
Gordon Jenkins

7 Heavenly

• Album sales: 1,000,000 │ **• Highest position:** 1 │ **• Release date:** August 1959 │

Released in 1959, *Heavenly* was Johnny Mathis' tenth album in just three years and the most successful of his standard album releases – its sales were exceeded only by his 1958 *Merry Christmas* album and a later compilation of his greatest hits.

Heavenly didn't succeed by doing anything patricularly innovative, but simpy by giving the public exactly what they had come to expect from Mathis, by now an established star. That meant a selection of show tunes, some standards and a smattering of new material, all delivered in the utterly relaxed Mathis tenor.

The title track was an early composition from the writing team of Burt Bacharach and Hal David. Another successful track was the vocal version of Errol Garner's jazz classic 'Misty', to which Mathis had added new lyrics by Joe Burke. 'Misty' went on to become Johnny Mathis' first hit single in two years.

Heavenly may have been more of the same as far as critics were concerned, but with this album Mathis appeared to have got the balance just right. The public responded with great enthusiasm, and Mathis was rewarded with five weeks at Number One. It went on to spend a remarkable five-and-a-half years in the charts.

Number One singles: None	**Recorded in:** New York, USA
Grammy awards: None	**Personnel:** Johnny Mathis
Label: US: Columbia; UK: Embassy	**Producer:** Mitch Miller

1 Heavenly (3:23)
2 Hello, Young Lovers (4:18)
3 Lovely Way To Spend An Evening (4:04)
4 Ride On A Rainbow (4:11)
5 More Than You Know (4:18)
6 Something I Dreamed Last Night (4:32)
7 Misty (3:38)
8 Stranger In Paradise (4:06)
9 Moonlight Becomes You (4:06)
10 They Say It's Wonderful (3:33)
11 I'll Be Easy To Find (4:04)
12 That's All (3.46)

Total album length: 48 mintues

Johnny Mathis

JOHNNY MATHIS
HEAVENLY

HEAVENLY
HELLO, YOUNG LOVERS
A LOVELY WAY TO
SPEND AN EVENING
A RIDE ON A RAINBOW
MORE THAN YOU KNOW
SOMETHING I DREAMED
LAST NIGHT

MISTY
STRANGER IN PARADISE
MOONLIGHT BECOMES YOU
THEY SAY IT'S WONDERFUL
I'LL BE EASY TO FIND
THAT'S ALL

Gunfighter Ballads And Trail Songs

| • **Album sales:** 2,000,000 | • **Highest position:** 6 | • **Release date:** September 1959 |

Marty Robbins already had a reputation for versatility in 1959 – he had recorded straight country, smooth pop, novelty songs and even some gentle rock 'n' roll – but when he cut his classic album of Western songs he surprised everyone. The cowboy song had had its heyday years before when the likes of Gene Autry had ruled the airwaves, and was generally seen as hopelessly out of date.

Robbins nursed a secret passion for this music, however, and had quietly composed a whole set of cowboy songs of his own. One afternoon in Nashville he went into the studio and recorded them all, aided and abetted by his back-up singers (later stars in their own right) brother Jim and Tompall Glaser. The result was that this side project became by far the biggest-selling album of Robbins' career. Its phenomenal success began with the release of the single 'El Paso' which, despite being four-and-a-half minutes in length, was an immediate hit, reaching number one on both pop and country charts.

The album soon followed suit and went on to become the definitive cowboy album – the aural equivalent of the classic TV series of the era, *Bonanza* or *Gunsmoke*. Robbins won a Grammy for Best Country and Western Performance for 'El Paso' in 1960.

Number One singles:
US: El Paso

Grammy Awards: Best country & western performance – El Paso

Label: US: Columbia; UK: CBS

Recorded in: Nashville, USA

Personnel:
Marty Robbins (d. 1982)
Thomas Grady Martin
Jack H. Prett
Bob Moore
Louis Dunn
Jim Glaser
Tompall Glaser

Producer:
Don Law

1   Big Iron (3:58)
2   Cool Water (3:11)
3   Billy The Kid (2:21)
4   A Hundred And Sixty Acres (1:42)
5   They're Hanging Me Tonight (3:06)
6   Strawberry Roan (3:25)
7   El Paso (4:21)
8   In The Valley (1:51)
9   The Master's Call (3:07)
10 Running Gun (2:12)
11 Down In The Little Green Valley (2:30)
12 Utah Carol (3:15)

Total album length: 35 minutes

GUNFIGHTER BALLADS
AND TRAIL SONGS

MARTY ROBBINS

Big Iron ★ Cool Water ★ Billy the Kid
A Hundred and Sixty Acres ★ They're
Hanging Me Tonight ★ The Master's Call
The Strawberry Roan ★ Running Gun
El Paso ★ In the Valley ★ Utah Carol
The Little Green Valley

PHOTO: DON CRAVENS OF BLACK STAR

5 Merry Christmas

• **Album sales:** 2,000,000 | • **Highest position:** 3 | • **Release date:** 1958 |

Over a 50-year career in the music business, Johnny Mathis recorded an extraordinary nine Christmas albums, but this, his first venture into seasonal recording, remains the best loved. At the time of the recording Mathis was aged 23 and the hottest young crooner in the business. He'd just made his film debut, appearing as a nightclub singer and a Christmas album was an obvious next move for Mathis.

For the album he was paired up with the legendary arranger Percy Faith and his orchestra. The material they chose was mostly of the tried and tested variety: Bing Crosby's 'White Christmas' is here, as is Nat King Cole's signature 'Christmas Song'. However, Mathis managed to find a signature tune of his own as well with the opening 'Winter Wonderland'.

The result was an album that has continually sold for more than 40 years, to the point where for many Americans it's an integral part of the Christmas experience. As Oprah Winfrey has said 'If you don't have Johnny Mathis, you don't have Christmas', while Mathis himself jokes that 'The only thing I'm not so fond of at Christmas is hearing myself so much.'

Number One singles: None	**Recorded in:** N/A
Grammy awards: None	**Personnel:** Johnny Mathis The Percy Faith Orchestra
Label: US: Columbia/CBS; UK: Fontana	**Producer:** Percy Faith

1 **Winter Wonderland (3:18)**
2 **Christmas Song (4:18)**
3 **Sleigh Ride (3:01)**
4 **Blue Christmas (3:02)**
5 **I'll Be Home For Christmas (4:06)**
6 **White Christmas (2:32)**
7 **O Holy Night (4:36)**
8 **What Child Is This? (4:00)**
9 **First Noel (3:50)**
10 **Silver Bells (3:34)**
11 **It Came Upon A Midnight Clear (3:11)**
12 **Silent Night (3:55)**

Total album length: 44 minutes

Johnny Mathis

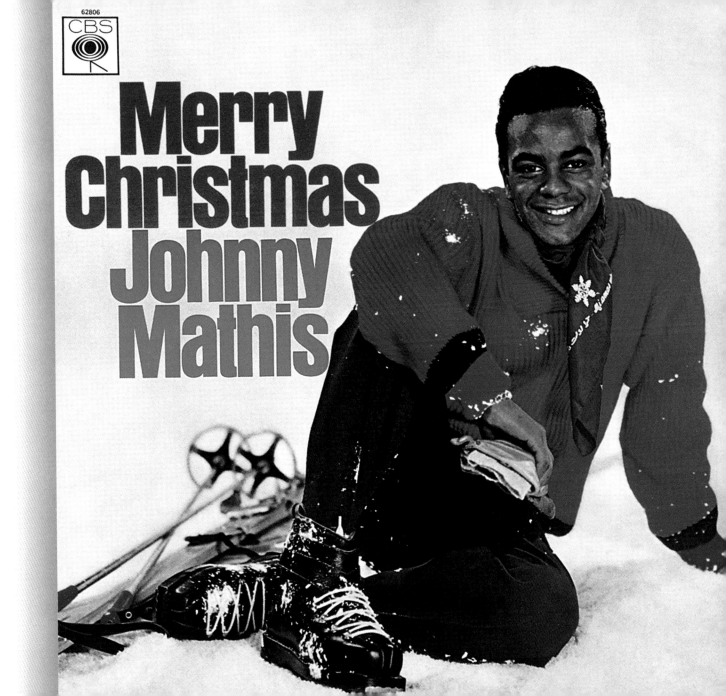

Oklahoma!

• **Album sales:** 2,000,000 | • **Highest position:** 1 | • **Release date:** August 1955

*O*klahoma! the movie arrived 12 years after the opening of the Broadway show. Based on *Green Grow The Lilacs*, the public were still entranced by Rodgers and Hammerstein's first work together and what became a landmark musical. The accompanying soundtrack to the movie sold 2,000,000 copies.

Composer Richard Rodgers and lyricist Oscar Hammerstein had a remarkable degree of control over the film version, ensuring that Hollywood remained faithful to the original work. Only two of the original songs ('Lonely Room' and 'It's a Scandal! It's a Outrage!') were missing from the two-and-a-half-hour movie, and Jay Blackton

continued to conduct. The orchestrations of arranger Robert Russell Bennett were recorded in stereo (as opposed to the mono recording of the Broadway cast album), giving the lush musical arrangements a breadth and depth that has continued to impress listeners. Complementing the sweeping orchestrations were the voices of the cast, all of them chosen as much for their vocal talent as for their box-office pull as movie stars. Gordon MacRae took the male lead role, while 20-year-old Shirley Jones played the female lead. Gloria Grahame took the role of Ado Annie. Their confident singing added warmth, intimacy and character to the lavish production.

Number One singles:
None

Grammy awards: None

Label: US & UK:
MCA/Capitol

Recorded in: N/A

Producer:
Ron O'Brien

Personnel:
Shirley Jones
Gordon MacRae (d. 1986)
Gloria Grahame
Rod Steiger (d. 2002)
Charlotte Greenwood
Gene Nelson
James Whitmore
Jay Blackton
Robert Russell Bennett

1 Overture (4:52)
2 Oh, What A Beautiful Morning (2:36)
3 The Surrey With The Fringe On Top (4:53)
4 Kansas City (2:36)
5 I Cain't Say No (3:10)
6 Many A New Day (3:09)
7 People Will Say We're In Love (4:21)
8 Pore Jud Is Daid (4:16)
9 Out Of My Dreams (2:25)
10 The Farmer And The Cowman (2:58)
11 All Er Nothin' (2:59)
12 Oklahoma! (3:18)

Total album length: 42 minutes

Original Soundtrack

From the Sound Track of the Motion Picture

Rodgers and Hammerstein's

3 Kind Of Blue

• **Album sales:** 3,000,000 │ • **Highest position:** No chart position │ • **Release date:** August 1959 │

Recorded in just two days, *Kind Of Blue* is not only the best-selling jazz album of all time, but also one of the most influential. It's likely to be the only jazz album that many rock fans have in their collection, and more than 40 years after its release, its reflective, sparse style is still considered modern.

The recording of *Kind Of Blue* was sandwiched in between two of Davis' big band projects: *Porgy And Bess* (which won a Grammy award for Best Soundtrack) and *Sketches Of Spain*. For *Kind Of Blue*, Davis assembled a small combo featuring pianist Bill Evans, whose input here is almost as great as that of Davis

himself, and legendary saxophonists John Coltrane and 'Cannonball' Adderley, who improvise superbly around the haunting modal themes and the crack rhythm section of Chambers and Cobb. The sessions were unrehearsed and spontaneous; Jimmy Cobb later remarked that the resulting recording was 'made in heaven'.

On release, the album sold respectably for a modern jazz record, but didn't enter the mainstream charts. However, with each passing year its reputation grew, to the extent that it now sells at least 5000 copies a week in the US, and has sold more than 5,000,000 copies worldwide.

Number One singles:
None

Grammy Awards:
None

Label: US: Columbia;
UK: Fontana

Recorded in: Columbia
30th Street Studio, New
York, USA

Personnel:
Miles Davis (d. 1991)
John Coltrane
Julian 'Cannonball'
 Adderley
Bill Evans
Paul Chambers
Jimmy Cobb
Wynton Kelly

Producer:
Irving Townsend

1   **So What** (9:25)
2   **Freddie Freeloader** (9:49)
3   **Blue In Green** (5:37)
4   **All Blues** (11:35)
5   **Flamenco Sketches** (9:25)

Total album length: 45 minutes

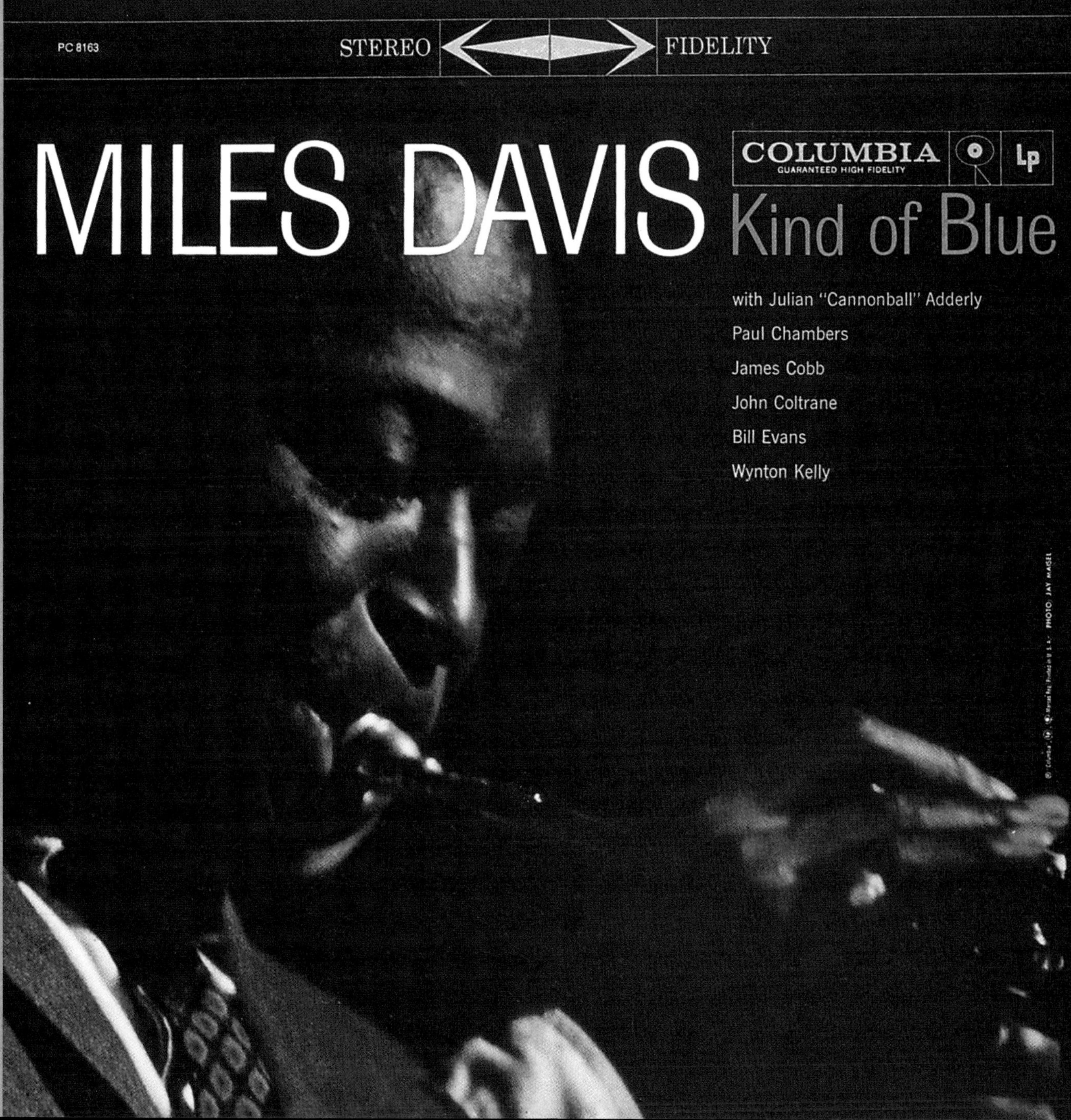

STEREO ◆ FIDELITY

MILES DAVIS

COLUMBIA LP
GUARANTEED HIGH FIDELITY

Kind of Blue

with Julian "Cannonball" Adderly

Paul Chambers

James Cobb

John Coltrane

Bill Evans

Wynton Kelly

Sleeve artwork by Joy Maisel

PHOTO: JAY MAISEL

My Fair Lady

| • **Album sales:** 3,000,000 | • **Highest position:** 1 | • **Release date:** March 1956 |

This recording of Lerner and Loewe's *My Fair Lady* was performed by the original stage cast, and on its release in 1956 topped the Billboard charts for 292 weeks – a record that to this day has not been broken.

The stage musical had been a huge success, running for 2,700 performances. It was considered superior to the average Broadway show: based on George Bernard Shaw's *Pygmalion*, Alan Jay Lerner's lyrics retained much of Shaw's wit and sparkle, while Frederick Loewe's songs ranged from the romantic ('I Could Have Danced All Night' and 'On The Street Where You Live') to the humorous ('The Rain In Spain' and 'Get Me To The Church On Time'). Few musicals can boast as many classic numbers. The original cast featured 22-year-old Julie Andrews (Eliza Doolittle) on top vocal form, Rex Harrison (Henry Higgins) perfecting his urbane 'talk singing' style, and Stanley Holloway (Alfred P. Doolittle) adding a touch of English music-hall comedy to the proceedings.

Not surprisingly, Broadway fans consider this original mono recording of the stage musical to be fresher than the technically polished recording of the 1964 film, in which Audrey Hepburn played Eliza, with vocals dubbed on by Marni Nixon.

Number One singles:
None

Grammy awards:
None

Label: US: Columbia;
UK: Philips

Recorded in: London, UK

Personnel:
Julie Andrews
Rex Harrison (d. 1990)
Stanley Holloway (d. 1982)
Gordon Dilworth
John Michael King
Philippa Bevans

Producer:
Goddard Lieberson

1 **Overture** (2:59)
2 **Why Can't The English** (2:40)
3 **Wouldn't It Be Loverly** (3:55)
4 **With A Little Bit Of Luck** (3:55)
5 **I'm An Ordinary Man** (4:38)
6 **Just You Wait** (2:41)
7 **The Rain In Spain** (2:39)
8 **I Could Have Danced All Night** (3:28)
9 **Ascot Gavotte** (3:13)
10 **On the Street Where You Live** (2:56)
11 **You Did It** (4:25)
12 **Show Me** (2:10)
13 **Get Me To The Church On Time** (2:42)
14 **A Hymn To Him** (3:28)
15 **Without You** (2:01)
16 **I've Grown Accustomed To her Face** (5:14)

Total album length: 53 minutes

Original Cast Recording

COLUMBIA MASTERWORKS   A HIGH FIDELITY RECORDING **LP**

Herman Levin presents

REX HARRISON
JULIE ANDREWS
MY FAIR LADY

adapted from Bernard Shaw's "Pygmalion"

book and lyrics by: **Alan Jay Lerner**
music by: **Frederick Loewe**
production staged by: **Moss Hart**

choreography and musical numbers by: Hanya Holm
production designed by: Oliver Smith
costumes designed by: Cecil Beaton

musical director/Franz Allers
orchestrations/Robert Russell Bennett
dance music arrangements/Trude Rittman
lighting/Feder

with **Stanley Holloway**

Robert Coote
Michael King / Rod McLennan

produced for records by Goddard Lieberson

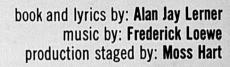

Elvis' Christmas Album

| • **Album sales:** 7,000,000 | • **Highest position:** 1 | • **Release date:** October 1957 |

Recorded in 1957, Elvis' first album of Christmas songs helped to establish him the king of light entertainment as well as rock-n-roll. Despite causing uproar on its release (Irving Berlin, the composer of 'White Christmas' led a campaign to stop Elvis' version being played on radio), the album hit Number One on the Billboard chart and continued to sell in large numbers each Christmas until 1962. Since then, it has become a Christmas classic, and is now the best-selling album of the 1950s.

The album, along with other material, was recorded in three days (September 5th–7th) at Radio Recorders in Hollywood. It contained a mixture of hymns, gospel tunes and secular Christmas songs, all of which Presley handled with characteristic panache. During the sessions, songwriters Leiber and Stoller wrote the opening track 'Santa Claus Is Back In Town', which became one of the collection's highlights.

On its release in October, media pundits, churchmen and music industry figures – knowing nothing of Presley's southern gospel roots – denounced it as an attempt by the young rock'n'roll rebel to profane Christianity. The public felt differently, however, and the album's obviously heartfelt religious spirit helped confirm Presley's status as an all-American folk hero.

Number One singles:
None

Grammy awards: None

Label: US & UK: RCA

Recorded in: Hollywood, USA

Personnel:
Elvis Presley (d. 1977)
Scotty Moore
Bill Black
DJ Fontana
The Jordanaires
Millie Kirkham

Producer:
Steve Sholes

1 **Santa Claus Is Back In Town** (02:12)
2 **White Christmas** (02:44)
3 **Here Comes Santa Claus (Right Down Santa Claus Lane)** (01:56)
4 **I'll Be Home For Christmas** (01:55)
5 **Blue Christmas** (02:08)
6 **Santa Bring My Baby Back (To Me)** (01:52)
7 **Oh Little Town Of Bethlehem** (02:37)
8 **Silent Night** (02:25)
9 **Peace In The Valley** (3:22)
10 **I Believe** (2:05)
11 **Take My Hand, Precious Lord** (3:21)
12 **It Is No Secret (What God Can Do)** (3:52)

Total album length: 30 minutes

Elvis Presley

Elvis' Christmas Album

plus a booklet of full colour photos

Appendix: Facts and figures

Grammy winning albums in the Top 100

1 *The Music From Peter Gunn*: Henry Mancini (19)
2 Grammys: Album of the year; Best arrangement

2 *Come Dance With Me*: Frank Sinatra (35)
2 Grammys: Album of the year; Best vocal performance

3 *Gunfighter Ballads & Trail Songs*: Marty Robbins (6)
1 Grammy: Best country & western performance

4 *The Music Man*: Original Cast Recording (9)
1 Grammy: Best original cast album (Broadway or TV)

5 *At Large*: The Kingston Trio (18)
1 Grammy: Best performance – folk

6 *The Lord's Prayer*: The Mormon Tabernacle Choir (29)
1 Grammy: Best vocal group/chorus

7 *The Kingston Trio*: The Kingston Trio (30)
1 Grammy: Best country & western performance

8 *Belafonte At Carnegie Hall*: Harry Belafonte (38)
1 Grammys: Best engineering contribution

9 *Gigi*: Original soundtrack (67)
1 Grammy: Best soundtrack album

10 *Tchaikovsky: Piano Concerto No.1*: Van Cliburn (69)
1 Grammy: Best classical performance – instrumental

Albums containing Number One singles

1 *The Unforgettable Nat King Cole*: Nat King Cole (14)
2 Number Ones: Mona Lisa; Too Young

2 *Gunfighter Ballads & Trail Songs*: Marty Robbins (6)
1 Number One: El Paso

3 *Elvis Presley:* Loving You (20)
1 Number One: Teddy Bear

4 *Elvis Presley*: King Creole (80)
1 Number Ones: Hard Headed Woman

Christmas albums in the Top 100

1 *Elvis's Christmas Album*: Elvis Presley (1)
2 *Merry Christmas*: Johnny Mathis (*9*)
3 *The Star Carol*: Tennessee Earnie Ford (12)
4 *A Jolly Christmas From Frank Sinatra*: Frank Sinatra (13)
5 *Chistmas Sing-Along With Mitch*: Mitch Miller And The Gang (28)
6 *Merry Christmas*: Bing Crosby (31)
7 *Christmas Carols*: Mantovani (45)
8 *Christmas Hymns And Carols*: The Robert Shaw Chorale (50)
9 *Christmas With Conniff*: Ray Conniff (64)

Movie and TV soundtracks in the Top 100

1 *Oklahoma!*: Various Artists (4)
2 *South Pacific*: Various Artists (15)
3 *The Music From Peter Gunn*: Henri Mancini (19)
4 *Porgy And Bess*: Various Artists (57)
5 *Gigi*: Various Artists (67)
6 *The Eddie Duchin Story*: Carmen Cavallaro (76)
7 *The Man With The Golden Arm*: Various Artists (78)
8 *King Creole*: Elvis Presley (80)
9 *Pal Joey*: Frank Sinatra (84)
10 *Peter Pan*: Various Artists (90)
11 *Deep In My Heart*: Various Artists (91)
12 *High Society:* Various Artists (92)
13 *Miss Showbusiness*: Judy Garland (96)
14 *Picnic*: Various Artists (96)
15 *There's No Business Like Showbusiness*: Various Artists (98)

Stage musicals in the Top 100

1 *My Fair Lady*: Various Artists (2)
2 *The Music Man*: Various Artists (9)
3 *The Sound Of Music*: Various Artists (17)
4 *Flower Drum Story*: Various Artists (27)
5 *West Side Story*: Various Artists (48)
6 *Damn Yankees*: Various Artists (97)
7 *Fanny*: Various Artists (100)

Record labels with the most albums in the Top 100

1 Capitol (30 albums)
2 Columbia/CBS (24 albums)
3 RCA/RCA Victor (21 albums)
4 Decca (12 albums)
5 Philips (4 albums)
6 Dot (3 albums)
7 Fontana (3 albums)
8 HMV (3 albums)
9 Kapp (3 albums)
10 London (2 albums)
11 MGM (2 albums)
12 Embassy (1 album)
13 Imperial (1 album)
14 Liberty (1 album)
15 Mercury (1 album)

Producers with the most albums in the Top 100

1 Voyle Gilmour (11 albums)
2 Mitch Miller (10 albums)
3 Dave Cavanaugh (4 albums)
4 Henri René (4 albums)
5 Steve Scholes (4 albums)

Artists with the most albums in the Top 100

(artists ranked by number of albums and aggregate score of album positions)

1 **Frank Sinatra:**

A Jolly Christmas From (13)
Sings Only For The Lonely (25)
Come Dance With Me (35)
Songs For Swinging Lovers (37)
Come Fly With Me (72)
In The Wee Small Hours (77)
No One Cares (79)
A Swinging' Affair (83)
Pal Joey (84)
Where Are You (86)

2 **Harry Belafonte:**

Calypso (16)
Belafonte (24)
An Evening With (34)
At Carnegie Hall (38)
Sings Of The Caribbean (85)
Mark Twain And Other Folk Favorites (87)

3 **Johnny Mathis:**

Christmas Album (5)
Heavenly (7)
Warm (36)
Open Fire, Two Guitars (41)

Swing Softly (52)
Wonderful, Wonderful (89)

4 **Mitch Miller And The Gang:**

Sing Along With Mitch (23)
Christmas Sing Along With Mitch (28)
Still More Sing Along With Mitch (42)
More Sing Along With Mitch (43)
Party Sing Along With Mitch (54)
Folk Songs Sing Along With Mitch (62)

5 **Mantovani:**

Film Encores (32)
Christmas Carols (45)
Gems Forever (46)
Strauss Waltzes (56)
Song Hits From Theatreland (58)
Mantovani Stereo Showcase (95)

6 **Elvis Presley:**

Elvis' Christmas Album (1)
Loving You (20)
Elvis Presley (21)
Elvis (26)
King Creole (80)

Appendix

7   The Kingston Trio:

At Large (18)

Here We Go Again (22)

The Kingston Trio (30)

From The Hungy I (39)

8   Tennessee Earnie Ford:

Hymns (11)

The Star Carol (12)

Nearer The Cross (47)

Spirituals (51)

9   Jackie Gleason:

Music For The Love Hours (63)

Lonesome Echo (74)

Romantic Jazz (81)

Music To Remember Her (94)

8   Roger Williams:

Till (44)

Songs Of The Fabulous Fifties (53)

More Songs Of The Fabulous Fifties (61)

The 10 highest-ranking solo artists

1   Elvis Presley: *Elvis' Christmas Album* (1)

2   Miles Davis: *Kind Of Blue* (3)

3   Johnny Mathis: *Merry Christmas* (5)

4   Marty Roberts: *Gunfighter Ballads And Trail Songs* (6)

5   Dave Brubeck: *Time Out* (10)

6   Tennessee Earnie Ford: *Hymns* (11)

7   Frank Sinatra : *A Jolly Christmas From* (13)

8   Nat King Cole: *Love Is The Thing* (14)

9   Harry Belafonte: *Calypso* (16)

10 Henry Mancini: *The Music From Peter Gunn* (19)

Groups and choirs in the Top 100

1   The Kingston Trio: *At Large* (18)

2   The Mormon Tabernacle Choir: *The Lord's Prayer* (29)

3   The Robert Shaw Chorale: *Christmas Hymns and Carols* (50)

Artists in the Top 100 not born or raised in the USA

1   Mantovani: *Film Encores* (32) (Italy/UK)

2   Antal Dorati: *Tchaikovsky's 1812* (40) (Hungary)

3   Crazy Otto: *Crazy Otto* (75) (Germany)

Index

Index

Index